A CURIOUS COLLECTION OF DANGEROUS CREATURES

AN ILLUSTRATED ENCYCLOPEDIA

SAMI BAYLY

THE EXPERIMENT

NEW YORK

CONTENTS

INTRODUCTION

This is not your average book of animals! It is my mission to shine a light on the more misunderstood species in the animal kingdom—as I did in my first book, *A Curious Collection of Peculiar Creatures*—and few have such unfair reputations (or are as unfairly treated) as the world's most dangerous animals. Because they can pose a threat to us, they are too often seen as something to fear or kill; instead, I'd like to show off how fascinating they are. Some are truly terrifying, yes, but if you understand *why* they've adapted to be so dangerous, you'll learn to appreciate their scarier sides. They're only trying to survive!

Here, you'll discover mind-blowing facts about fearsome animals as well as many you probably didn't even know were deadly. And, hopefully, you'll grow to appreciate them for their unique contributions to the natural environment.

Every one of these 60 animals is a brilliant combination of strange and dangerous, and I loved painting them and their quirky attributes in watercolor. I hope I have showcased their true magnificence.

Sami Bayly

AFRICAN BUFFALO

Syncerus caffer
(sin-seer-us caf-er)

*T*hese enormous animals can grow as tall as 6 feet (1.8 m) and weigh as much as 2,000 pounds (900 kg). You can honestly say they weigh a ton! Their most unique feature is their curving horns, which look like a funny hairstyle. Both females and males have horns, and a male's horns can measure up to 4 feet (about 1.25 m) from tip to tip. These horns aren't just for decoration—they can also be used as weapons.

Danger Factor

The African buffalo belongs to a group in Africa called "The Big Five," alongside the lion, rhinoceros, elephant, and leopard. These are the animals known to be the most dangerous to humans. Despite their size, African buffalo can run as fast as 35 miles (57 km) per hour. When they feel threatened, they charge directly at the threat, using their large horns to toss the victim into the air.

Conservation Status

NEAR THREATENED

Even though these creatures are considered extremely dangerous to humans, humans can also be extremely dangerous to them. Humans hunt them for sport and meat, but the bigger threat is to their habitat, which humans use for their own needs. In the 1800s, the African buffalo was threatened by an infectious disease called "rinderpest," which greatly reduced its population. Today, it is estimated that there are about 56,000 African buffalo.

What They Eat

You might think that an animal this large and deadly eats a lot of other animals. But African buffalo are actually herbivores, which means they don't eat meat. Instead, they mostly graze on leaves and grasses. A buffalo eats mainly at night. After it finishes eating, it brings its partially digested meal, called "cud," back up into its mouth and chews it slowly during the day.

Where They Live

African buffalo make their homes in the lowland rain forest, grasslands, and woodlands of the sub-Saharan region of Africa. Their habitat must have a constant source of water and supply of grasses and leaves for the herd to survive. They live and travel in groups of several hundred, which provides safety in numbers but can be life-threatening for any animal caught in the way of a stampede.

FUN FACTS

◆ Don't make an enemy of the African buffalo. They have good memories and have been known to attack hunters who harmed them several years before.

◆ African buffalo have a unique relationship with a bird called the oxpecker, which rides on the buffalo's back and eats the ticks, lice, and fleas it finds crawling there. The oxpecker even eats the buffalo's earwax! Scientists are still trying to decide if this relationship is helpful or semiparasitic.

◆ African buffalo have smooth tongues, unlike cows, whose tongues can be as rough as sandpaper.

AFRICAN GIANT SWALLOWTAIL

Papilio antimachus
(pap-ill-e-o anti-mak-us)

The African giant swallowtail is the largest butterfly in Africa and one of the largest in the world, so these insects are often mistaken for birds when they are flying. Their narrow orange and black wings can measure from 7 to 10 inches (17 to 25 cm) tip to tip. That means their wingspan is almost as long as an unsharpened pencil!

Danger Factor

As well as being large, these butterflies are very poisonous. Scientists believe that during the caterpillar stage, the African giant swallowtail eats leaves that are full of toxins called "glycosides," which become even more dangerous as they are digested. This means that when the butterfly emerges from its chrysalis, it will be deadly to any predator that consumes it.

Conservation Status

DATA DEFICIENT

It is very unusual to see an African giant swallowtail in the wild, and so there is not enough data to know its conservation status. Because other animals, such as birds, have learned how deadly they are and know not to eat them, humans are the only danger these insects face. Their habitat is threatened by humans, and the butterflies are often illegally captured and sold to collectors, who want to display their magnificent wings.

What They Eat

Scientists think that the poisonous leaves the African giant swallowtail eats during its caterpillar stage are from the climbing oleander, a plant with white, pink, and purple flowers. The toxins from this innocent-looking plant stay in the butterfly's system until adulthood and make it poisonous. Once the caterpillar becomes a butterfly, it eats flower nectar.

Where They Live

African giant swallowtails live in the rain forests of west and central Africa. Males stay close to the ground, usually near water, but females spend all of their time high in the tree canopy. The butterflies are difficult to find, and the caterpillars are even more so. Scientists still don't know what the African giant swallowtail actually looks like during the caterpillar stage.

FUN FACTS

◆ The African giant swallowtail must have a very strong stomach. Scientists believe that the toxins in climbing oleander leaves are so strong they could kill a hippopotamus (found on page 40)!

◆ The first recorded European sighting of an African giant swallowtail was in 1782.

◆ Besides being poisonous to eat, African giant swallowtails possess another defense mechanism: they release a cloud of stinky chemicals when disturbed.

AFRICANIZED BEE

Apis mellifera scutellata Lepeletier

(ay-pis mel-if-er-a skew-tell-a-ta lep-el-et-ee-er)

What happens when an African honeybee and a European honeybee mate? You get a hybrid called the Africanized bee! These flying insects have a fuzzy exoskeleton made up of three parts. The head contains the brain, eyes, antennae, and two mandibles. The middle section is called "the thorax," where the bee's four wings and six legs attach. And the third part, the abdomen, is where the stinger is found. Not much bigger than a dime, these brown bees with black stripes measure from one half to three quarters of an inch (about 1.25 to 2 cm).

Danger Factor

Nicknamed "killer bees," Africanized bees first appeared in Brazil, where it is estimated that about 1,000 people who were allergic to bees have died from their stings. Africanized bees will defend their nest from any threat and have been known to swarm and chase trespassers as far as a quarter mile (almost 0.5 km), delivering hundreds of stings. But to label them "killer bees" is not fair—after all, they are simply defending their hive.

Conservation Status

NOT EVALUATED

The Africanized bee is now considered to be an invasive species. Africanized bees first appeared in the 1950s, when African honeybees were brought to Brazil to help increase honey production and a number of swarms mated with the local European honeybee population. It is likely that this species will continue to spread, as these bees are very good at adapting to their environment.

What They Eat

Africanized bees eat nectar and pollen, which they transform into honey. They are incredible pollinators, which makes them valuable and useful members of their environment. They are also very important to humans because they pollinate many of the crops of fruits and vegetables that humans eat.

Where They Live

Since first appearing in the South American country of Brazil, Africanized bees have slowly spread throughout many parts of South America and all of Central America. They are even making their way up to North America. These bees build nests in all sorts of places, both outdoors and indoors, including woodpiles, tree hollows, logs, chimneys, and roofs.

FUN FACTS

◆ Can you count to 1,000? That's how many Africanized bee stings it would take to kill an adult who doesn't have a bee allergy.

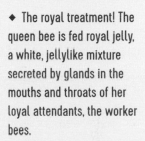

◆ The royal treatment! The queen bee is fed royal jelly, a white, jellylike mixture secreted by glands in the mouths and throats of her loyal attendants, the worker bees.

◆ If you are running away from a swarm of Africanized bees, don't try to escape underwater, as they will wait for you to surface.

ALLIGATOR SNAPPING TURTLE

Macrochelys temminckii

(macro-chel-ees tem-in-key-eye)

With its spiky shell, scaled tail, and sharp beak-like jaws, the alligator snapping turtle might make you think that dinosaurs still roam the earth. Their name comes from the ridges on their shells, which look like an alligator's skin. The largest freshwater turtles in North America, the males can weigh between 155 and 175 pounds (70 to 80 kg). That's a lot to fit into a 26-inch-long (66 cm) shell! The females are smaller, weighing an average of 50 pounds (23 kg).

Danger Factor

As its name says, the alligator snapping turtle "snaps" its sharp jaws shut on nearby prey or anything that poses a threat. If you meet one, keep your fingers away from its jaws! Scientists measured the alligator snapping turtle's bite force and found that these turtles chomp down with the strength of 1,000 pounds (450 kg), or the weight of a large piano. That is enough to go through bone!

Conservation Status

VULNERABLE

These turtles' habitats are threatened by pollution and overcrowding, and they are hunted by humans for their meat and shells. It is especially important to protect these turtles because they play an important role in the environment by eating decomposing animals and plants. Maintaining the population size of the species is essential to their survival, as well as to the quality of their ecosystem.

What They Eat

This omnivore lies motionless at the bottom of the water with its mouth open, wiggling its pink tongue. Just like a worm on a hook, the tongue attracts fish, as well as frogs and mollusks. The turtle's algae camouflage allows it to slowly sneak up on its prey: small birds, mammals, and even other turtles! It can snap smaller prey clean in half or swallow it whole.

Where They Live

Alligator snapping turtles make their homes in freshwater biomes such as lakes, rivers, and other salt-free bodies of water in the southeastern US. They are hard to spot in the wild because they hide behind leaves and vines and under fallen logs and rocks, and they can hold their breath underwater for up to 50 minutes! About once a year, the females leave the water to lay their eggs on land.

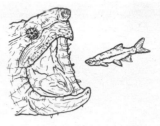

FUN FACTS

◆ You may have seen a turtle hide its head in its shell. Alligator snapping turtles cannot hide this way because they are not able to retract their bulky heads.

◆ In captivity, alligator snapping turtles can live up to 70 years, but those in the wild usually live for only 11 to 45 years.

◆ The collective name for these animals is a "dole" or "bale."

ASIAN GIANT HORNET

Vespa mandarinia

(ves-pa man-dar-in-e-a)

About the length of a fun-size candy bar, the Asian giant hornet can grow up to 2 inches (5 cm) long, making it the world's largest wasp. But there's nothing sweet about it! With its spiked mandible, large eyes, and 3-inch (7.5 cm) wingspan, this is one scary-looking insect! Its stinger is almost a quarter inch (a little more than 0.5 cm) long, and it is this stinger that makes the Asian giant hornet so dangerous.

Danger Factor

The Asian giant hornet's nickname is "the murder hornet." Its sting is very painful, and the toxins in its venom can cause allergic reactions in humans and sometimes even death. But it is not humans who are most in danger from these wasps. The Asian giant hornet attacks honeybees, biting off their heads and feeding their bodies to its young. One hornet can kill about 40 bees in a minute, and an entire honeybee colony can be destroyed in hours.

Conservation Status

NOT EVALUATED

Many people consider the Asian giant hornet a nuisance and an invasive species, but humans are more of a threat to it than it is to us. In Japan, where the hornet is most commonly found, people deep-fry them, like french fries, and eat them. Can you imagine eating a wasp? Scientists also worry that the hornet population will decline as its forest habitat is destroyed.

What They Eat

Asian giant hornets are fierce predators and use their jaws rather than their stinger to catch prey. They hunt insects such as beetles, hornworms, bees, and other wasps. They also eat tree sap and fruit.

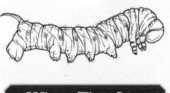

Where They Live

As its name suggests, the Asian giant hornet lives in Asia, particularly the southeastern and eastern areas. It makes its home in the temperate and tropical forests of countries like China and Japan. The hornets usually dig subterranean nests that can be up to 2 feet (60 cm) deep in the ground, but sometimes they use nests that mice and rats built.

FUN FACTS

◆ Unlike most honeybees, the Asian giant hornet does not lose its stinger and die after just one sting. It can use its stinger over and over again. Ouch!

◆ The Japanese honeybee has learned how to fight back against attacks by the Asian giant hornet. The honeybees swarm a single hornet, creating a "bee ball," and beat their wings so fast it creates heat, which cooks the hornet to death.

◆ Asian giant hornets are believed to live for only around 3 to 5 months.

◆ The first sighting of an Asian giant hornet in North America was in Canada in 2019. It is thought that this wasp hitched a ride on a shipping container.

AUSTRALIAN MAGPIE

Gymnorhina tibicen

(gym-nor-ina tib-i-sen)

Look out! The Australian magpie is famous for swooping in on anyone who comes too close to its nest. Recognizable by its distinctive black-and-white feathers, this magpie also has a warble that sounds like flute! An adult Australian magpie is about 16 inches (40 cm) tall and weigh a little more than half a pound (300 g). With its long legs, it doesn't waddle or hop, like other birds, but walks quickly when chasing prey.

Danger Factor

Australian magpies are very protective parents and will do almost anything to keep their newly hatched babies safe. Male Australian magpies have been to known to swoop, squawk, claw, and peck at anyone they feel is too close to their hatchlings, sometimes inflicting severe eye and face wounds. It's important to be alert to their unique song, wear sunglasses and a hat to protect your eyes and head, and keep an eye on the birds, since they often attack when their victim's back is turned.

Conservation Status

LEAST CONCERN

The Australian government protects this native species with laws to prevent it from being killed or having its eggs taken by humans. Thanks to this, the Australian magpie has a large population size, which is predicted to increase. Predators such as foxes, cats, and dogs are the biggest threat to these birds.

What They Eat

Australian magpies are omnivores, which means they eat everything! They feed on critters like insects, spiders, worms, and snails, and occasionally feast on slightly larger animals, such as lizards and frogs. They also eat grain, figs, and nuts. They typically search for their food on the ground.

Where They Live

The Australian magpie can make itself at home almost anywhere! It lives in temperate grasslands, tropical forests, and savannas, but it also lives in cities. Like its name suggests, the Australian magpie can be found throughout Australia, as well as in parts of southern New Guinea. Its ability to nest just about anywhere is the reason so many people are affected by its defensive parenting.

FUN FACTS

◆ Australian magpies are nicknamed "flute birds" because of their magnificent call. They can also mimic the sounds of other birds, horses, dogs, and sometimes even humans!

◆ If you meet an Australian magpie, be sure to be nice. These birds can recognize faces, and they have great memories, often recalling those who treated them well and those who did not.

◆ Australian magpies sometimes lie in the dirt with their wings outstretched. But they are not injured or sick—they are sunning themselves in order to remove unwanted parasites.

BIBRON'S STILETTO SNAKE

Atractaspis bibronii
(at-rack-tas-pis bib-roni-eye)

Bibron's stiletto snakes are approximately 12 to 16 inches (30 to 40 cm) long, though some grow as big as 31 inches (80 cm)! Because they are a solid gray, brown, or black color, they can look like a very long worm or a nontoxic snake. But don't be fooled into picking one up! After the Mozambique spitting cobra and the puff adder, the stiletto snake causes the third-highest number of serious snakebites in South Africa.

Danger Factor

This snake is named after a long, thin knife—a "stiletto"—because of its long, thin fangs, which inject venom into their victims. Although their venom is not usually deadly to humans, it can cause severe pain, swelling, tissue damage, and, in some cases, the loss of fingers. The Bibron's stiletto snake also has a sharp spike at the end of its stubby tail, which it will press into a hand that reaches for it. If you come across a stiletto snake, the best way to keep this from happening is to leave it alone.

Conservation Status

NOT EVALUATED

These snakes spend most of their time underground, and so it is rare to come across them in the wild. They are also sometimes mistaken for other snakes. For these reasons, the conservation status of the Bibron's stiletto snake is not entirely known. Fortunately, scientists think these snakes do not face many threats from predators, nor do people want to have them as pets!

What They Eat

Like stealthy assassins, Bibron's stiletto snakes use their sharp fangs to stab their prey and inject them with venom. This carnivorous snake hunts other underground animals, such as lizards, frogs, rodents, and even other snakes.

Where They Live

Bibron's stiletto snakes can be found in grasslands, savannas, and lowland forests throughout much of South Africa, Namibia, Eswatini, and Botswana. They spend most of their time underground, but they sometimes emerge in the early evening when it is warm or after a heavy rain.

FUN FACTS

◆ These snakes have a funny smell that may help them attract a mate or scare a predator.

◆ There is no antivenom medicine for the bite of a Bibron's stiletto snake. The only treatment is to try to reduce the pain and wait.

◆ Don't try to sneak up on a Bibron's stiletto snake! They can rotate their fangs and turn their heads to bite a sneak attacker.

◆ These snakes' fangs stick out of the corners of their mouths, so they don't even have to open their mouths to bite!

BLACK MARLIN

Istiompax indica

(is-tee-om-pax in-di-ka)

eady, set, go! Able to swim as fast as a cheetah can run, up to 80 miles (128 km) per hour, the black marlin is one of the ten fastest animals in the world. Given its speed, you might expect it to be small, but this monstrous fish can grow to a whopping 15 feet (4.5 m) long and weigh up to 1,650 pounds (750 kg). Over millions of years, its unique features, such as its extremely long bill that looks like a sword, have evolved to help it hunt and survive, making it a dangerous underwater predator.

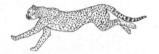

Danger Factor

At the top of the food chain, these giant fish are apex predators, which means they have no natural animal predators. While they mostly use their swordlike bills to catch prey, they have been known to impale fishers after being captured and pulled onto boats. And on rare occasions, they've even impaled divers who were swimming too close.

What They Eat

This meat-eating fish feasts on a variety of sea creatures, including squid, octopus, cephalopods, crustaceans, and small tuna. Scientists determined that the fish uses its long, sharp bill to stab and cut its prey before consuming it.

Where They Live

Black marlins like warm, salty water and live mostly in the Indian and Pacific Oceans. They can be found as deep as 3,000 feet (915 m) but usually hang out in water that is up to 100 feet (30 m) deep. They like to live close to reefs and land masses.

Conservation Status

DATA DEFICIENT

The biggest threat to the black marlin is humans who catch it to sell it for food or keep it as a trophy. Recreational fishers enjoy the challenge of catching this large, speedy fish. It is also often caught accidentally by tuna-fishing ships. Conservationists do not have enough information to know whether the black marlin is threatened by overfishing.

FUN FACTS

◆ Female marlins grow faster and larger than the males and live almost twice as long.

◆ Just like trees, black marlins have rings that can tell you how old they are. These growth rings are found in a spine in the marlin's dorsal fin.

◆ Black marlins can swim for very long distances. Scientists tracked two marlins who swam from the coast of Australia to the coast of India—a distance of almost 5,000 miles (8,000 km)!

BLACKLEGGED TICK

Ixodes scapularis
(ix-o-dees scap-you-lar-is)

Even though they are only the size of a sesame seed, blacklegged ticks can cause an incredible amount of pain and suffering. Ticks are members of the arachnid family, meaning they are related to spiders (like the Brazilian wandering spider on page 30 and the red-headed mouse spider on page 94) and scorpions (like the Indian red scorpion on page 72). Because they are so small, they are often difficult to spot, and they can hide in areas of the body such as the armpit, groin, and scalp.

Danger Factor

With their sharp, pointed teeth, blacklegged ticks attach themselves to humans and animals, or "hosts." Some of these ticks carry Lyme disease, which they can give to their host through their bite. If these ticks are not removed within 36 to 48 hours of biting a person, that person's risk of being infected with Lyme disease gets bigger. When blacklegged ticks infect other animals, it can cause paralysis, meaning the animal can't move. If a large group of ticks feeds on one animal, that animal may die.

Conservation Status

NOT EVALUATED

The blacklegged tick is thriving, because its habitat has plenty of its most favorite host: deer (another name for this creature is "deer tick"). It does not have many predators, but it is a valuable food source for a variety of creatures, including guinea hens and opossums. Climate change will probably be the biggest challenge to the blacklegged tick's future survival.

Where They Live

Blacklegged ticks live within the northeastern, north-central, and mid-Atlantic regions of the United States. They hang out wherever they can find their favorite hosts—deer, rodents, dogs, and humans—and are most commonly found in deciduous forests.

What They Eat

During its approximately two-year life span, the blacklegged tick consumes only three meals. Each meal lasts from three to five days and provides enough energy to fuel each stage of its life cycle after hatching: larva, nymph, and adult. Larvae and nymphs tend to feed on small rodents. Adults prefer white-tailed deer.

FUN FACTS

◆ Blacklegged ticks will sit on tall grass or leaves with outstretched front legs, waiting for a ride. This is called "questing." When a host brushes by, the tick climbs onboard.

◆ Safety first! If you've been playing in the woods, ask your adult to check for ticks afterward. And don't forget to check your four-legged family members as well.

◆ Your chance of catching Lyme disease depends on three factors: what species the tick is, where it was before it bit you, and how long it was feeding on you.

0.7–0.15 inches (2–4 mm)

BLUE DRAGON

Glaucus atlanticus

(glaw-kuss at-lan-tik-uss)

Only about 1 inch (3 cm) long, the blue dragon (not actually a dragon, but a kind of sea slug) floats upside down in the ocean with its blue belly facing upward, so it will blend in with the water when seen from above. Its submerged silver back helps it blend in with the sea surface when seen from underneath. This fantastic adaptation is known as "countershading" and keeps it safe from predators both above and below.

Danger Factor

Blue dragons aren't naturally venomous, but they eat venomous creatures. After many meals, a blue dragon builds up enough toxin in its body to unleash a mighty sting against any predators. These stings can hurt not only other sea creatures but also humans. Stings to humans can be incredibly painful, causing welts, swelling, increased heart rate, and vomiting, so it's important to resist touching these beautiful dragons!

What They Eat

The blue dragon eats only jellyfish, both big and small ones, such as the Portuguese man o' war and the blue button. Despite its own small size and slow movement, the blue dragon is a fierce predator and can hunt prey that has tentacles up to 30 feet (9 m) long. It uses its knifelike jaws to clamp down on its victim.

Where They Live

Blue dragons especially like the warm, tropical waters of the Pacific, Indian, and Atlantic Oceans. They are most often found on the surface of the water, but they can dive much deeper and live anywhere from the floor of an ocean to its surface.

Conservation Status

NOT EVALUATED

Because this tiny dragon lives in a vast area of the ocean, it is quite tricky for scientists to know the range and population of the species. Their movements are controlled by the weather and the waves, and so they are often thrown about by storms and washed up on the beach, but it is thought that their numbers are still high.

FUN FACTS

◆ Have you ever held a beach ball close to your stomach while floating in a pool? The blue dragon swallows air, making a bubble like a beach ball in its stomach. This is what keeps it afloat.

◆ Blue dragons are hermaphrodites, which means an individual can produce both sperm and eggs; however, another blue dragon is still needed for fertilization of the eggs.

◆ The blue dragon is also called a "sea angel," and a group is called a "blue fleet."

◆ While it is pretty to look at, the blue dragon does not make a good pet, not only because of its sting but also because you can't buy its food at a pet supply store!

BLUE-AND-YELLOW MACAW

Ara ararauna
(air-a are-a-raw-na)

A harmful bacterium called *Chlamydia psittaci* can be found on the blue-and-yellow macaw, and it's this bacterium (not the macaw) that's really dangerous. The tiniest known living organisms, bacteria are everywhere, including inside humans. They are so tiny that they can be seen only through a microscope. Many types are helpful, but some types can make a person, or a pet, sick.

Danger Factor

Besides making a bird sick, this bacterium can be transmitted through its droppings, which, when dry, turn into dustlike particles that can be inhaled by humans. A person can then develop an infectious disease called "psittacosis," or "parrot fever." The effects of psittacosis vary from a mild illness to more severe flu-like symptoms. If not treated properly, it may cause death.

Conservation Status

NOT EVALUATED

Since *Chlamydia psittaci* is not an animal or plant, it cannot be given a conservation status. But this bacterium can spread very quickly. Outbreaks are most common in places where birds are kept in cages. People such as vets, zookeepers, bird owners, and people who work in pet shops and the poultry industry can help prevent the spread of the bacterium by washing their hands with antibacterial soap, wearing a mask, and cleaning the birds' cages and food and water bowls daily.

What They Eat

All living things, even tiny organisms like bacteria, need to eat. *Chlamydia psittaci* absorbs nutrients from its host in order to gain the energy it needs to reproduce.

Where They Live

Chlamydia psittaci lives in the lungs. This bacterium is not picky and lives in many species of birds, including chickens, ducks, and turkeys, but it especially likes pet birds from the parrot family, like parakeets, African grey parrots, and, of course, the blue-and-yellow macaw.

FUN FACTS

◆ You may know a bird is infected if it displays inflamed eyes, low appetite, diarrhea, and trouble breathing. However, not all infected birds show symptoms.

◆ Older than dirt! Bacteria have been around for over 3 billion years, making them the oldest living organisms.

◆ Catching psittacosis once will not prevent you from catching it again. You can contract the disease as many times as you are exposed to it. So always wash your hands after touching a bird or cleaning a birdcage.

BOOMSLANG

Dispholidus typus
(dis-foe-lid-us tie-pus)

Reaching a whopping 5 feet (1.5 m) in length, boomslang snakes are swift and slender. The females are often a dull green, brown, or gray color. The males are a much more vibrant light green with blue or black scales. The boomslang's keyhole-shaped eyes work something like binoculars, giving them excellent eyesight.

Danger Factor

Like many snakes, the boomslang is venomous. Its venom prevents normal blood clotting, which means its victim will continue to bleed both inside and outside the body after being bitten. Without medical help, a person who has been bitten by a boomslang snake could die. Luckily, these snakes are very shy and avoid people.

Conservation Status

NOT EVALUATED

The boomslang snake is not vulnerable or endangered. Its most common predators are mongooses and birds of prey, such as falcons and ospreys. But thanks to its well-camouflaged body and fast moves, scientists suspect that these snakes are successful in avoiding most predators. Its biggest enemy is humans, who kill it out of fear.

What They Eat

This sneaky snake darts through tree branches, remaining hidden in order to hunt. Using its camouflage, the boomslang snake will hide in a tree and strike out when its prey approaches, rarely leaving without a meal. These carnivores eat eggs, birds, lizards (including chameleons), frogs, and other snakes.

Where They Live

Native to Africa, the boomslang snake can be found in savannas and lowland forests throughout the continent, including southern and central areas such as Zimbabwe, Botswana, and Namibia. They are arboreal reptiles, which means they live in short trees and shrubs that help them to stay hidden. Occasionally, they will venture to the ground to sunbathe or hunt.

FUN FACTS

◆ Open wide! Boomslang snakes' fangs are at the back of their mouths. In order to inject venom, they must open their jaws 170 degrees. That is almost a straight line from top to bottom!

◆ When a boomslang snake feels threatened, it makes its body into an "S" shape and gets ready to strike.

◆ The boomslang is one of a few snake species that can fold its fangs back into the roof of its mouth after using them!

BRAZILIAN WANDERING SPIDER

Phoneutria nigriventer
(phone-a-tree-a nig-riv-en-ter)

With eight long legs that can reach up to 6 inches (15 cm) across when it walks, the Brazilian wandering spider is one of the most venomous spiders on Earth. These hairy spiders are often brown with a black spot on their stomach. They also have eight eyes and red jaws, and they look especially frightening when they're in defense mode, raising their two front legs and showing their fangs.

Danger Factor

This spider's bite is very painful and can cause serious symptoms, such as trouble breathing and paralysis, which is when you can't move. But it will only bite or attack if it is aggravated or scared. And its bite is not usually deadly. Instead of using all of its toxic venom in one bite, the spider releases just enough to stop an attacker. This clever survival strategy lets it save some venom to continue to protect itself while it replenishes its supply.

Conservation Status

NOT EVALUATED

During the day, this spider hides in dark places, and at night it travels across the forest floor. This makes it very difficult for scientists to study and count them, and for this reason, the conservation status of the Brazilian wandering spider is unknown. In some countries, you can keep one as a pet if you have a Dangerous Wild Animals license.

What They Eat

The Brazilian wandering spider does not weave webs, so it must catch its meals another way. Like its name suggests, it "wanders" the forest floor throughout the night, hunting prey. Its carnivorous diet includes other spiders and insects and sometimes even small reptiles, mice, and frogs.

Where They Live

You won't find these spiders in a house. They live in the jungles of Central and South America. Though sometimes they accidentally hitch a ride to Europe or North America in a crate of bananas!

FUN FACTS

◆ There are actually eight species of the Brazilian wandering spider, and the kind that usually travels in bananas is harmless. They're also known as "banana spiders" because they like to hide among the fruit.

◆ When attempting to mate, the males "dance" for the females, who are quite picky and reject many suitors before choosing a mate. Then the "lucky" male is often attacked after mating!

◆ The Brazilian wandering spider lives for just one to two years.

◆ Their species name, *Phoneutria*, is the Greek word for "murderess."

BULLDOG ANT

Myrmecia pyriformis
(mer-mee-see-uh pure-uh-for-miss)

According to *Guinness World Records*, the bulldog ant, known for its aggressive behavior, is the most dangerous ant in the world. If one of these inch-long (2.5 cm) ants gets cut in half, its two halves attack each other! With its large, toothed mandible, the head bites the tail. And with its venom-filled stinger, the tail attacks the head. These reddish-brown insects are very tough!

Danger Factor

The bulldog ant has no fear of humans, and it can sting multiple times, releasing more venom with each jab. They use their mouthparts, or mandibles, to grip their victim, while jabbing their stinger, located at the tail end of their body, into the victim multiple times, delivering a load of venom. The effect of the sting is usually pain, but it can also cause an extreme allergic reaction, and even death. The ant's venom can paralyze smaller creatures, allowing the ant to eat them without having to hold them in place.

What They Eat

As larvae, bulldog ants eat a carnivorous diet of small insects, including other ants. They are fed by the worker ants, who use their stingers to paralyze prey and their large mandibles to carry it back to the colony. The adults are mostly herbivores and consume nectar, fruit, seeds, honeydew, and fungi.

Conservation Status

NOT EVALUATED

The bulldog ant's primary threat is from predators such as wasps, other spiders, and birds. Despite their aggressive and dangerous behavior, bulldog ants are important to the environment because they aerate the soil when creating underground tunnels, they eat decaying leaves and animals, and they are an essential food source within their ecosystems.

Where They Live

Bulldog ants make their nests underground on the eastern side of Australia. Using a tunnel system, they build their colonies in woodland and eucalyptus forest areas. They can also be found in cities. It is relatively easy to see them once you start looking, as their mounds and quick-moving bodies are easy to spot.

FUN FACTS

◆ The bulldog ant can kill a human in just 15 minutes.

◆ Rather than having one brain, bulldog ants have several "mini brains," or ganglia, throughout their body. The one in their head controls senses, such as sight and smell, and the others control movement.

◆ This species of ant is as old as the dinosaurs! Scientists believe that ants have existed for 140 million years and that the bulldog ant first appeared around 100 million years ago.

CANE TOAD

Rhinella marina
(ri-nella mar-ina)

These large amphibians are 4 to 6 inches (10 to 15 cm) long. When they are young, they have smooth skin that is usually a dark color. Adult toads have dry, light brown or yellow skin and are covered in bumpy glands that look like warts. No, you can't catch warts from a toad, but you still shouldn't touch these dangerous animals!

Danger Factor

Cane toads are poisonous. They are harmful to people and animals who touch, lick, or eat them. Their poison can make a person's eyes and skin burn, but it is much more harmful to animals, causing heart problems, shaking, and even death. This means that cane toads not only kill their predators but can also hurt and kill innocent pets. Curious cats and dogs who lick the toad can be poisoned.

Conservation Status

LEAST CONCERN

While they do face some natural predators, including crows, tawny frogmouths, wolf spiders, and water rats—as well as humans, who hunt and use their skin to make bags, souvenirs, and medicine—the cane toads' population and range are rapidly increasing across places like Australia and Florida, where they are considered an invasive species. There is an effort to control their population growth for the sake of the animals that the cane toad negatively affects, such as dingoes, freshwater crocodiles, and red-bellied black snakes.

What They Eat

These omnivores are rarely short on food because they are not picky eaters! They enjoy insects, small birds, frogs, lizards, small mammals, snakes, and plants.

Where They Live

The cane toad's preferred habitat is usually tropical but can be semiarid (or dry), though they have also adapted to living in open woodlands and grasslands. Cane toads used to live only in the Americas, but now they can be found in places as far away as Australia, Japan, the Philippines, and Papua New Guinea.

FUN FACTS

◆ One of the cane toad's predators, the Australian native water rat, uses surgical precision to remove the toad's poisonous glands and feeds only on the surrounding heart or liver.

◆ In 1935, 102 cane toads came to Australia. Today, scientists estimate that there are over 1.5 billion toads living there!

◆ The Chocó Indians of western Colombia "milked" cane toads by draining their poison into a bottle. Then they smeared the milky poison onto the tips of the arrows and blow darts they used for hunting.

CHIMPANZEE

Pan troglodytes
(pan trog-low-die-ts)

We share more than 97 percent of our DNA with this wonderful primate. Scientists believe that humans and chimpanzees have a common ancestor who lived between 7 and 13 million years ago. When standing on two legs, a chimpanzee can be close to 5 feet (1.5 m) tall, and their weight ranges between 60 and 150 pounds (27 to 68 kg). They have long arms and fingers, plus opposable thumbs and big toes that help them move quickly through the trees.

Danger Factor

A male chimpanzee is five times as strong as a human. They can be very violent toward other male chimps, both while roughhousing and asserting dominance. Baby chimps are often kept as pets, both legally and illegally, around the world. But cute and playful infants grow into strong adults who are very smart and become bored in a human environment, which can lead to destructive behavior.

Conservation Status

ENDANGERED

Sadly, these tree-loving primates are losing their habitats to deforestation. They're also threatened by hunters, who poach them for meat and trap them to sell as pets. The third danger they face: diseases that also affect humans. In 2002, the Ebola virus killed large numbers of the Central African chimpanzee.

What They Eat

With their long fingers, thumbs, and opposable big toes, chimpanzees use "utensils" to eat! Chimpanzees are omnivores, which means their diet is packed with both plants and animals. Some foods they enjoy are small mammals, birds, eggs, insects, fruits, leaves, seeds, and flowers. Their large teeth not only help them to eat these foods but also help them to express their emotions!

Where They Live

Chimpanzees live in 21 countries all over the continent of Africa, mostly in the tropical rain forest belt of Central Africa but also in woodlands and grasslands. They live in groups of approximately 35, including both males and females. Most chimpanzees sleep in nests they build in the treetops, where the cozy leaves and high branches keep them safe from predators.

FUN FACTS

◆ Humans are so similar to chimps that you could even receive a blood transfusion from one, as long as you shared the same blood type.

◆ Chimps spend a lot of time "grooming" each other—picking out lice, dandruff, and dirt with their long fingers. This not only keeps them clean but also makes them better friends!

◆ These apes are believed to use herbal medicine. Sick chimps have been observed eating certain medicinal plants.

COFFIN RAY

Hypnos monopterygius

(hip-noss monop-ter-ij-ee-us)

The coffin ray has minuscule eyes, a large mouth filled with up to 60 rows of tiny teeth on top and bottom, and a row of five gill slits on the underside of its body. It likes to bury itself in the sandy ocean floor, which makes it difficult to breathe through these gills, so it also has spiracles, or tiny round openings, just below its eyes.

Danger Factor

Zap! The coffin ray has a secret weapon. Located on either side of its head are organs that generate an electrical charge. Coffin rays use this charge to stun prey and defend themselves from predators. This adaptation delivers a powerful shock to anything that touches the ray, sending up to 200 volts into its victim—enough to numb the affected area! The ray's most common human victims are divers who accidentally touch or step on them.

Conservation Status

LEAST CONCERN

The coffin ray is quite abundant throughout its habitat. People don't find them tasty to eat, so they are not threatened by commercial or recreational fishing. Occasionally, they are accidentally captured by large fishing boats, but in most cases they survive this adventure since they can live out of water for hours at a time and are usually thrown back into the sea.

What They Eat

Coffin rays are carnivores. They use their electricity to stun fish, crabs, and worms. The ray's mouth is located on the underside of its body and can stretch wide enough to eat prey half its size! It attacks quickly, swallows the prey headfirst, and then buries itself in the sand.

Where They Live

Native to Australia, coffin rays can be found around much of the Australian coast in subtropical and temperate waters. They like to hide anywhere from 260 to 650 feet (80 to 200 m) underwater, in the sandy and muddy bottoms of beaches, bays, and estuaries. They have also been found hanging out near coral reefs and resting under sea grass. While they are quite tricky to spot, a sharp eye may spy the raised shape of their bodies buried in the sand.

FUN FACTS

◆ Coffin rays are typically a little over 1 foot long, or about 15 inches (40 cm).

◆ Some have been found with penguins in their bellies!

◆ They're also known as "numbfish" because their electrical charge causes numbness.

◆ Coffin rays often wash up on the beach with the tide. The unlucky ones who don't catch a wave home become dried out, bloated, and "coffin" shaped.

COMMON HIPPOPOTAMUS

Hippopotamus amphibius

(hippo-pot-a-mus am-fib-e-us)

Growing up to 16 feet (almost 5 m) long and 5 feet (1.5 m) tall and weighing nearly 3,000 pounds (almost 1,400 kg), the common hippopotamus is the third-largest land mammal. It is also considered semiaquatic, because it spends up to 16 hours a day standing with its eyes, ears, and nose peeking above the waterline. Hippos even give birth in the water, and babies can weigh up to 77 pounds (35 kg).

Danger Factor

Sometimes called a "water horse," the common hippopotamus is a fierce animal. It has giant jaws that open almost into a straight line. This lets it show off its large teeth, which can grow over 1 foot (30 cm) long. Hippos are aggressive and will charge any threat to their territory, including humans. They have attacked people in boats and on land, and they kill hundreds of people every year in Africa. So be sure to admire them from a safe distance!

Conservation Status

VULNERABLE

The common hippopotamus is listed as vulnerable for two reasons: extreme habitat loss and hunting. People hunt hippos for food, and trophy hunters kill them for their huge ivory teeth, which they can sell for a lot of money. But the number of wild hippopotamuses has stayed steady in the 21st century, and national parks provide protected habitats, such as the rivers that keep these hippos happy and safe.

What They Eat

Hungry, hungry hippos! You might think they would use their 1.5-foot-long (50 cm) tusks for feasting on large mammals, but these herbivores eat grass, leaves, and plant shoots for 4 to 5 hours a night! They eat an average of 88 pounds (40 kg) of greens a day. That's a lot of salad!

Where They Live

Hippos live south of the Sahara desert, in countries like Ethiopia, Kenya, and Gambia. They make their homes in subtropical and tropical forests, moist savannas, shrublands, grasslands, and wetlands. They live in groups of 10 to 100 and spend their days together, wallowing in shallow lakes, rivers, and swamps.

FUN FACTS

◆ Hippos wag their tails to spray their droppings over a large area, to mark their territory and to attract a mate.

◆ The hippo is closely related to some ocean animals, including dolphins and whales.

◆ These hippos produce a reddish-brown oily acid that helps keep their skin moist and protects them from bacteria.

CROWN-OF-THORNS STARFISH

Acanthaster planci
(a-can-thast-er plank-eye)

Since starfish are not actually fish, marine scientists have started calling them "sea stars." At 9 inches (almost 23 cm) in diameter, the crown-of-thorns starfish is one of the largest sea stars—about the size and shape of a Frisbee. And like Frisbees, they come in many colors: red, orange, green, or purple, depending on their diet. They can have between 8 and 23 arms, which are covered in super-sharp, venomous, thornlike "spines" that can be up to 2 inches (5 cm) long.

Danger Factor

It's not their regenerating arms full of toxic spines that make this invertebrate dangerous. Instead, it's their large dinner parties. Crown-of-thorns starfish, or "COTs" for short, prey on coral polyps, the tiny organisms that make up coral reefs. When large groups of COTs (called an "outbreak") get together on the same part of a reef, they can permanently harm or kill it. In just one year, a single COTs can destroy up to 32 square feet (10 sq m) of precious reef, changing the ecosystem dramatically.

Conservation Status

NOT EVALUATED

Crown-of-thorns starfish are often referred to as an invasive species, and some governments believe that killing this sea star would protect reefs. But scientists know that smaller populations of COTs help reefs stay diverse and healthy. Human activities, such as overfishing, tourism, pollution, and climate change, hurt reefs as well. It is vital that we first reduce the human impact on reefs before eradicating a natural species.

What They Eat

When they are hungry, these corallivores find a section of coral, open their mouth, and their stomach pops out! The stomach attaches to the coral and releases digestive juices that suck out nutrients. All that is left behind is the white skeleton of the coral.

Where They Live

Crown-of-thorns starfish can be found living on reefs in tropical waters such as the Red Sea, the Indian Ocean, and the southern part of the Pacific Ocean. They are a common species on the Great Barrier Reef, located in the Coral Sea off the coast of Queensland, Australia.

FUN FACTS

◆ The crown-of-thorns starfish can regenerate, or grow back, an arm lost in an accident or fight within a few months!

◆ Despite their prickly exterior, their natural predators include the giant triton snail and the titan triggerfish (see page 118).

◆ Female COTs can release up to 65 million eggs per year. That's a lot of tiny stomachs to feed!

◆ Crown-of-thorns starfish grow more arms as they age, and their life expectancy is up to 17 years.

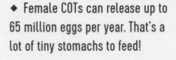

DEER MOUSE
Peromyscus maniculatus
(per-o-mi-scuss man-e-cule-at-us)

*E*xtremely tiny, at less than 4 inches (10 cm) long, the deer mouse can slip through the woodlands mostly unseen by humans. These quiet rodents are nocturnal, which means they are most active at night. Long whiskers, located next to their pointy snout, touch nearby objects and help deer mice to "see" the world around them, even in the dark. Large ears let them listen for predators.

Danger Factor

Some deer mice carry germs that cause a virus called "hantavirus," a serious sickness that makes it difficult to breathe. Humans can be infected by inhaling dust with particles of an infected mouse's droppings, urine, or saliva in it. It's important not to let mice build nests near your home. Always let an adult clean up mice nests and droppings. They can stay safe by wearing gloves and a face mask while doing this dirty job.

What They Eat

Always be prepared! These omnivores gather plants and insects both to eat now and to save for later. This foraging and storing of food lets them eat well during the colder times of the year. Seeds, nuts, fruits, and meaty insects are always on the menu!

Conservation Status

LEAST CONCERN

Due to its large population size and wide variety of habitats across North America, the deer mouse is considered of least concern. Deer mice are a very valuable part of our ecosystem. They help spread plant seeds throughout the forests and prairies. They are also an important part of the food chain and provide nutrition to carnivores such as owls, foxes, snakes, and coyotes.

Where They Live

Found throughout the United States, southern Canada, and central and northern Mexico, the deer mouse is the most common rodent in North America. It lives happily in a number of different habitats, including grasslands, woodlands, deserts, and agricultural fields, though it prefers the tree-filled forests and grassy prairies. It is when mice live close to humans—for example, nesting in the roofs and walls of homes—that they become dangerous.

FUN FACTS

◆ Baby deer mice, known as "pups," are hairless when born and don't open their eyes for about 15 days.

◆ Deer mice have been known to eat their own droppings—most likely to absorb the nutrients they lost the first time around.

◆ These mice have a special strategy for keeping warm. If the outside temperature drops too low, the mice lower their body temperature and enter a state of sleep known as "torpor." This helps them to survive during the cold winter months.

ELECTRIC EEL

Electrophorus voltai

(elec-tro-for-us volt-eye)

The electric eel is actually a fish in an eel costume. It is a type of knifefish and is not related to the eel. All three electric eel species have snakelike bodies that can grow up to 8 feet (2.5 m) long and weigh about 45 pounds (20 kg), and they can live for 10 to 22 years. About 80 percent of their body is made up of organs that produce electricity, so they produce an oily substance that protects them from their own electric charge!

Danger Factor

The *Electrophorus voltai*, also called a Volta's eel, currently holds the title for "strongest electrical discharge by an animal." It can shock its victim with 860 volts of electricity at once. That's approximately 200 more volts than the other two species of electric eel! If you accidentally touch a Volta's eel, you will get a serious zing, but you will live to tell the tale, although it is especially serious for people with heart conditions because of the possibility for heart and respiratory failure.

What They Eat

Baby electric eels will eat unhatched eggs, while young eels snack on invertebrates and insects found in the water. Adults eat a diverse variety of meat, including fish, crabs, small amphibians, reptiles, and mammals. Volta's eels sometimes hunt in groups. Together, the pack can put out a stronger electrical charge to stun their prey. Teamwork!

FUN FACTS

◆ Electric eels also use their electricity to locate prey underwater. They send out low pulses, which work as a radar system to track an upcoming meal.

◆ An adaptation allows electric eels to breathe air through their mouths when they surface above water. This also means they can survive in water that has low levels of oxygen.

◆ The female electric eels lays eggs in a nest of foam that the male creates with saliva.

Conservation Status

LEAST CONCERN

Scientists have evidence that electric eels have been around for millions of years. With such a strong defense system, they have very few natural predators. They are occasionally caught to be sold as pets, or collected for scientific research, but fortunately, this has very little impact on their population size.

Where They Live

All three species of electric eels call the South American Amazon and Orinoco River basins home. They inhabit swamps, creeks, and floodplains. The Volta's eel lives on the eastern side of South America, in an area called the Brazilian Shield. Its habitat has fast-moving water and waterfalls.

FLAMBOYANT CUTTLEFISH

Metasepia pfefferi

(met-a-seep-ee-a feff-er-ee)

O nly 3 to 4 inches (7 to 12 cm) in size, the flamboyant cuttlefish is poisonous. Luckily, a cuttlefish warns others about its poison. Its skin has special cells called "chromatophores" that allow the cuttlefish to change color. Normally, this dark brown cephalopod camouflages itself to blend in with its ocean-floor home. But when it feels threatened or excited, it pulses with color—bright yellow, red, pink, and orange—and black stripes move in waves along its body.

Danger Factor

Marine biologists observed that the flamboyant cuttlefish uses a warning system that is similar to those of other toxic animals. But they still didn't know if the cuttlefish was dangerous to predators, including humans. These scientists found that it does contain a small amount of a toxin that is also found in another cephalopod, the southern blue-ringed octopus (see page 110). But they haven't yet found evidence of the flamboyant cuttlefish harming other animals.

Conservation Status

DATA DEFICIENT

Even though scientists don't have enough information on the population size of the flamboyant cuttlefish, they do know that their habitat is threatened. Polluted oceans, overfishing, and rising levels of acid in the ocean water, caused by global warming, are problems for all marine life.

What They Eat

Flamboyant cuttlefish eat mostly bony fish and crustaceans. They hunt along the ocean floor or near coral reefs, stalking their prey or luring it in with their bright colors. These small carnivores are very successful predators!

Where They Live

Found in the tropical waters around Australia, New Guinea, and the islands of the Philippines, Indonesia, and Malaysia, the flamboyant cuttlefish lives on sandy and muddy seafloors. Although it can be found at depths ranging from 9 to 282 feet (3 to 86 m), it prefers shallow waters.

FUN FACTS

◆ Now you see it, now you don't! The flamboyant cuttlefish can "disappear" by releasing an inky cloud when threatened. This cloud confuses a predator and gives the cuttlefish time to escape.

◆ These cuttlefish live for around 1.5 to 2 years.

◆ The white, chalky back end of a cuttlefish, known as a "cuttlebone," is often spotted washed up on beaches. These are given to pet birds because they are packed with calcium and help strengthen the birds' beaks.

GEOGRAPHY CONE SNAIL

Conus geographus

(cone-us geog-raf-us)

There's more to the geography cone snail than meets the eye! It may look like a beautiful, harmless seashell, but tucked inside this 4- to 6-inch (10 to 15 cm) brown-and-white shell is the world's most venomous sea snail. It uses a large, flat body part called a "foot" to slowly walk along the ocean floor. When the cone snail senses prey nearby, it extends its long, tubelike organ called a "proboscis," which contains a sharp hollow tooth that the snail uses to harpoon and inject venom into its prey. It can do this to anything that makes it feel threatened, including a human hand.

Danger Factor

Although the sting of a geography cone snail feels as mild as a bee sting, it is much more dangerous. It can cause a person to stop breathing and even die within just an hour. One shot of this snail's venom is enough to kill up to 15 people, but there have been only 36 reported deaths in 300 years.

Conservation Status

LEAST CONCERN

Currently, conservationists are not worried about the geography cone snail's survival. It lives in a wide range of locations, and because of its highly venomous nature, it has few natural predators. Future threats to the cone snail might emerge if it is overharvested, either for its magnificent shell or for scientific research.

What They Eat

Unlike other members of the cone snail species, the geography cone snail is a piscivore, meaning it mostly eats fish. Preferring to hunt at night, it releases insulin into the surrounding water. The insulin causes blood sugar levels in nearby fish to drop, and they lose energy. The snail then injects its sluggish target with venom. Finally, it pulls its entire meal into its shell. Hours later, it spits out the fish bones.

Where They Live

To encounter one of these saltwater dwellers, you need to swim near coral reefs, in shallow waters in the Indo-Pacific region, or along the coast of Australia. And you're more likely to see one at night. The geography cone snail is primarily nocturnal and buries itself under the sandy ocean floor to rest during the day.

FUN FACTS

◆ There is no antivenom for geography cone snails, so a person who is stung can only wait for the venom to leave their body.

◆ These snails can live to the ripe old age of 15 years.

◆ Scientists are studying how its toxins can create medicine that actually relieves pain, which could be very helpful to humans and might just change the cone snail's reputation!

GERMAN COCKROACH

Blattella germanica

(blat-tella germ-ani-ca)

At less than half an inch (1.2 cm) long, the German cockroach is one giant pest! Out of the world's 4,500 species of cockroach, this one is identified by its light brown color and two dark stripes running down the sides of its oval body. It also has a hard, flat covering on its back that protects it from being easily crushed. Six spiny legs help it to run quickly over land. Though it has wings, it never really learned how to fly. It uses two long antennae that extend from its head to feel and smell, and it frequently cleans them throughout the day—perhaps to better smell its next meal.

Danger Factor

It is not the German cockroach's bite or sting that makes it dangerous. They can be a health hazard to humans. Their discarded exoskeletons and bodily waste create a "dust," and humans can develop severe allergies and even asthma from this dust. German cockroaches can also carry and spread bacteria, which contaminates food and surfaces and may cause stomach illnesses.

Conservation Status

NOT EVALUATED

The German cockroach's conservation status is not known, but most people consider it a nuisance. This tough insect is a survivor that continually adapts to new threats. Its ability to reproduce incredibly fast and the fact that it has few predators might mean that the German cockroach will outlast all other living creatures on the planet!

What They Eat

Omnivorous scavengers, German cockroaches will eat anything! Decaying meat, rotten fruit, and discarded leftovers are all a part of a German cockroach's balanced diet. And if actual food is not available, they'll snack on soap and even toothpaste. Though they do seem to have a sweet tooth and prefer sugar and sweets.

Where They Live

Can you guess where the German cockroach comes from originally? Here's a hint: It's not Germany! German cockroaches are originally from Southeast Asia or northeastern Africa, but now they can be found across the globe. Anywhere where they have access to food and can hide in the dark and out of sight of passersby is prime cockroach real estate.

FUN FACTS

◆ German cockroaches can lay up to 40 eggs at a time, and they can live for up to 200 days.

◆ A German cockroach breathes through spiracles, or vents, on the sides of its body. This means that if it loses its head, it can continue to breathe!

◆ All cockroaches can run superhero fast. At top speed, they run a distance of 50 body lengths in just one second. And the German cockroach is even speedier than most other species of cockroach.

◆ Cockroaches roamed the earth with the dinosaurs. The oldest known cockroach fossil is 130 million years old.

◆ German cockroaches can so quickly infest an area because of their speedy reproduction rate and longevity: They can lay up to 40 eggs at a time, and they can live for up to 200 days.

53

GIANT OTTER

Pteronura brasiliensis

(terro-new-ra bra-sil-ee-en-sis)

Winning the prize for the largest otter in the world, the giant otter can weigh between 40 and 60 pounds (18 to 27 kg) and is 5 to 6 feet (1.5 to 1.8 m) long. Webbed feet, a strong tail, and the ability to plug its nose and ears to keep water out make it an excellent swimmer.

It also has a waterproof outer layer of brown fur. Giant otters live in family groups of three to eight members of different ages. Each otter has unique white markings on the fur of its throat, which allows them to recognize each other, and they're closely related to the wolverine (page 122).

Danger Factor

These carnivorous members of the weasel family are extremely territorial and very feisty. Utilizing their sharp teeth, powerful jaws, and intimidating claws, they will tear into anything that threatens them or their young, both natural predators and humans. They aren't afraid of some of the most feared animals in the world, such as the caiman, piranha, and anaconda. Luckily, they have no interest in us unless we pose a threat.

Conservation Status

ENDANGERED

From 1940 until 1973, humans hunted giant otters for their velvety soft fur pelts, which were used to make coats and hats. For this reason, the giant otter almost became extinct. Destruction of the giant otter's habitat is also a threat to its survival. Gold mining, logging, and overfishing all contribute to destroying their river habitats at an alarming rate, so much so that by 2045, their population may decrease by 50 percent or more.

What They Eat

Near the top of the food chain, the giant otter eats 6 to 9 pounds (2.7 to 4 kg) of food every day. Fish is its favorite meal, but it will also eat crabs, birds, turtles, and small reptiles. The giant otter does not have very good table manners. It rarely shares its food and it often eats its prey immediately.

Where They Live

A giant otter family uses fallen logs to create a roomy burrow along a riverbank in the moist, tropical forests of South America. The otter's ideal habitat is in large, slow-moving bodies of water. Aquatic biomes in the Amazon, Orinoco, and La Plata river systems provide leafy cover and shallow waters for hunting.

FUN FACTS

◆ These otters are known as apex predators, but on rare occasions, they've been observed falling prey to pumas and jaguars.

◆ Scientific research suggests that, at one time, they were even more giant, reaching almost 8 feet (2.4 m) long!

◆ The collective noun for otters in water is a "raft."

◆ "Ha!" No, the giant otter isn't laughing. It makes this noise to warn other otters of danger. It also barks, hums, and screams. Scientists have discovered that it uses 22 different noises to communicate everything from "What's up?" to "Hey, can I have some of your lunch?"

GILA MONSTER

Heloderma suspectum

(hello-derma sus-pect-um)

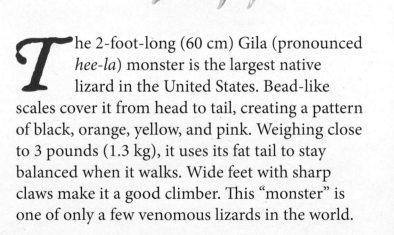

The 2-foot-long (60 cm) Gila (pronounced *hee-la*) monster is the largest native lizard in the United States. Bead-like scales cover it from head to tail, creating a pattern of black, orange, yellow, and pink. Weighing close to 3 pounds (1.3 kg), it uses its fat tail to stay balanced when it walks. Wide feet with sharp claws make it a good climber. This "monster" is one of only a few venomous lizards in the world.

Danger Factor

There are many tall tales about the Gila monster's fatal bite, venomous spit, and sneak attacks. But it is actually rather docile. It moves slowly and gives a warning hiss to threats. However, if you do get too close to one and are bitten, you are in store for a lot of pain! The Gila monster bites down with its grooved teeth to release its venom. Often, it will refuse to let go and needs to be forcibly removed. A person bitten by a Gila monster might vomit, faint, or get a fever, but there is no record of a Gila monster killing a human.

Conservation Status

NEAR THREATENED

This creature's biggest threat is habitat loss as humans clear its land for farms and highways. Humans also hunt them to sell as pets or kill them out of fear. Despite its dangerous reputation, the Gila monster became the first protected venomous animal in North America. In 1952, it became illegal to collect, kill, or sell Gila monsters.

What They Eat

The Gila monster mostly feasts on stolen bird and reptile eggs and rarely uses its venom to kill prey, which suggests that this weapon is mainly for defense. The Gila monster eats one third of its weight in one meal and stores fat in its plump tail. This means it needs to eat only four or five meals a year!

Where They Live

These bumpy lizards live throughout the southwestern United States and into northwestern Mexico. California, Nevada, Utah, New Mexico, and Arizona provide the best desert biomes for the Gila monster. When not sunbathing, it spends its time in an underground burrow.

FUN FACTS

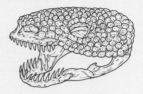

◆ Its beaded scales are actually tiny pieces of bone called "osteoderms" that are located under the skin. The Gila monster's scientific name, *Heloderma suspectum*, means "studded skin."

◆ Do you have any gum? A Gila monster's breath is so terrible that people used to believe it was deadly.

◆ Gila monsters, which typically live up to 8 years but can live to 20, are immune to their own venom.

GOLDEN POISON FROG

Phyllobates terribilis

(fill-o-bates ter-i-bil-us)

Golden poison frogs have three shiny colors: yellow, orange, and light green. These vibrant colors act as a warning to predators, letting them know that this animal is very dangerous. These tiny, 2-inch-long (5 cm) amphibians have four toes at the end of each leg and an extra bone in their jaw that can make it look as though they have teeth. They may resemble tiny, shiny toys, but they are actually the most poisonous vertebrates on Earth.

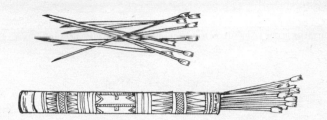

Danger Factor

A single lick of the golden poison frog can kill you, and its skin contains enough toxins to kill 10 to 20 humans. For centuries, tribes in South America coated the tips of darts with this poison to hunt small animals. This is why they are also called "poison dart frogs." No longer used for hunting, the golden poison frog is still treated with respect and fear. Just touching one can make you feel a burning sensation for hours!

Conservation Status

ENDANGERED

The Amazon rain forest that the golden poison frog calls home is slowly disappearing. Gold mines destroy the forests and pollute the rivers. Conservationists fear that there are only about 5,000 golden poison frogs left in the wild. Other human-related threats include the use of pesticides. But because these frogs are so toxic, they face very few natural predators.

What They Eat

Golden poison frogs have very long, sticky tongues, which they use to trap their insect prey in one quick motion! They eat ants, termites, crickets, flies, and beetles.

Where They Live

Found only in South America, golden poison frogs live in a small area of the Colombian rain forest. Since amphibians start their lives in water, they need fresh water nearby. They also need very humid habitats, as the mixture of heat and moisture is essential for their survival. The tropical forest provides a moist forest floor with small streams running through it. With its bright coloring, the golden poison frog can be easily spotted among the leaves.

FUN FACTS

◆ Golden poison frogs get their poison from eating a small species of beetle called a melyrid beetle, just like the hooded pitohui (page 68). When the frogs are collected and kept in captivity for a long period of time, they lose their toxicity because they are no longer eating the melyrid beetle.

◆ The male golden poison frog stores the female's eggs on his back to safely deliver them to the water for fertilization.

◆ Forward, march! The collective name for a group of frogs is an "army."

GOLIATH TIGERFISH

Hydrocynus goliath
(hydro-sin-us go-lie-ath)

"**G**oliath" is another word for "giant," and weighing in at around 110 pounds (50 kg) and measuring 5 feet (1.5 m) long, this fish has earned its name. Its 32 sharp interlocking teeth sit along the edge of its very powerful jaw. These teeth can grow up to 1 inch (2.5 cm) long and are visible even when the goliath tigerfish's mouth is closed! Sharp eyes peer out from this fierce river monster's dark silver body. These fish are often compared to piranhas (page 92) because of their size, the fact that they do not hunt in packs, and their ferocious nature.

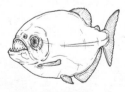

Danger Factor

With daggerlike teeth sharp enough to slice a fish clean in half, the goliath tigerfish could easily hurt a human. But while a few attacks have been reported, luckily, this fish doesn't crave humans for dinner. These attacks most likely happened when people attempted to catch it. When it comes to the goliath tigerfish, it is better to look with your eyes and not with your hands!

Conservation Status

LEAST CONCERN

Because of the goliath tigerfish's size and aggressive nature, it faces very few threats. Its only known animal predator is the Nile crocodile. Fishers will attempt to catch it, but if they do manage to snag this fierce creature, they often release it back into the wild. To maintain this fish's population and position within the ecosystem, humans should not disturb them.

What They Eat

This carnivore eats mostly fish. It lurks near fast-moving water, waiting for its next meal. Using its "ears" to detect vibrations in the water as well as its excellent eyesight, the goliath tigerfish tracks its prey. When it senses food nearby, it circles the prey until the fish becomes exhausted and slows down. Then, *snap!* The goliath tigerfish's jaws clamp down.

Where They Live

Found throughout central Africa, the goliath tigerfish is a freshwater fish, which means it lives in lakes and large rivers, primarily within the Congo River basin.

FUN FACTS

◆ The largest goliath tigerfish on record weighed 154 pounds (almost 70 kg).

◆ Unlike other fish in African waters, the goliath tigerfish is not afraid of crocodiles. There are even rumors that they eat small ones!

◆ May I have your autograph? The goliath tigerfish became a TV star when it was featured on the television program *River Monsters* in 2010. It took a 200-pound (91 kg) rod and an 8-hour struggle to capture a goliath tigerfish. Unfortunately, the fish was injured during its fight to stay in the water and so could not be released back into the wild. Instead, it was given to local villagers to eat.

GREATER SLOW LORIS

Nycticebus coucang

(nik-tis-bus cow-kang)

Have you ever spent a quiet day just hanging out by yourself, maybe enjoying a fruit snack? Then you know how the greater slow loris spends most of its time. Sometimes called shy, or malu-malu in Indonesian, this small tree-dweller is known for moving slowly and quietly through the forest. About 3 pounds (1.3 kg) and 15 inches (40 cm) from its head to its tail, the greater slow loris may look like an adorable stuffed animal, but it's a venomous primate with a toxic bite!

Danger Factor

You'll know a greater slow loris is about to strike because first it will raise its arms and lick its armpit. This may look like a strange dance, but it's how it collects its venom. The greater slow loris produces a toxin in the glands inside its elbows. When it grooms, or licks, itself, the toxin mixes with its saliva, creating an oil that collects in its front teeth, called a "toothcomb." That oil is powerful enough to cause an extreme allergic reaction that affects a person's breathing and could even kill them if they are not treated.

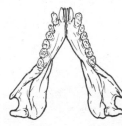

Conservation Status

ENDANGERED

Sadly, its cuteness factor has put the greater slow loris at risk. People take them from the wild and sell them as pets. They are also killed for their body parts, which are used illegally by people who believe their fur and skin can cure illnesses. Habitat loss and natural predators such as pythons, orangutans, and eagles also endanger the greater slow loris.

What They Eat

Greater slow lorises are mostly vegetarian, snacking on tree sap, tree gum, nectar, and fruit. Occasionally they add meat to their diet, getting some protein from eggs and snails. These creatures are nocturnal and wait until night to forage and eat their meals.

Where They Live

The greater slow loris lives in a variety of forest habitats throughout Malaysia, Indonesia, Singapore, and parts of Thailand. They are arboreal, living up in the trees and relying on their amazing climbing ability and grip to crawl from branch to branch. Although these primates are active only at night, it is possible to see them in the wild.

FUN FACTS

◆ Mother slow lorises lick their babies to coat them in venom, which protects them from predators.

◆ When threatened, the greater slow loris moves in a way that makes it look like a cobra snake. It has an extra vertebra in its spine, which lets it sway and strike like that deadly animal.

◆ Slow but steady! A greater slow loris can travel through close to 5 miles (8 km) of trees in one night.

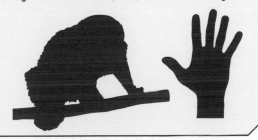

GREATER WEEVER FISH

Trachinus draco
(track-i-nuss dray-co)

The *draco* in the species name of the greater weever fish stands for "dragon," a surprising name for what, at first glance, appears to be an ordinary fish. Weighing about 2 pounds (almost 1 kg) and reaching an average length of 10 inches (25 cm), its greenish-brown body, dappled with darker brown stripes and orange speckles, is sometimes described as tigerlike. The greater weever fish has a "superior" mouth, which means that it opens upward because the lower jaw is longer than the upper jaw.

Where They Live

LEAST CONCERN

Once its dangerous spines are removed, the greater weever fish is not only edible but also quite tasty. Brave fishers catch and sell it to fish markets in southern Europe and Scandinavia and sometimes use it as bait to catch other fish. It is also caught accidentally by trawlers. Despite this, it is still abundant and widespread throughout its habitats.

This saltwater fish lives throughout the northeastern and central eastern Atlantic Ocean, as well as in the Black, Baltic, and Mediterranean Seas. It hangs out in water that is approximately 330 feet (100 m) deep and is not often seen by swimmers or fishers. Buried up to its eyes and dorsal fin in the sandy, muddy, or gravelly seabed, it protects itself from predators.

Danger Factor

If you accidentally catch a greater weever fish, don't touch it! This fish has a row of five to seven needlelike spines down its dorsal fin, as well as one on each side of its face, near its gills. These spines secrete a venom that is so strong it can cause a person to experience sharp pain, swelling, fever, nausea, vomiting, and dizziness. While no one has died from a greater weever fish's venom, people have died from infections related to being stung by one.

What They Eat

The greater weever fish likes to bury itself in the sand, up to the eyeballs on top of its head. It hides like this, lying in wait to ambush unsuspecting prey. Preferring to feed at night, it eats other small fish and crustaceans such as shrimp.

FUN FACTS

◆ The greater weever fish has an annoying little sibling named the lesser weever fish. Even though the lesser weever fish is smaller, its venom is more powerful than that of its big sibling!

◆ Its common name, "weever," comes from the Old French word "wivre," which means both "dragon" and "viper," like the snake.

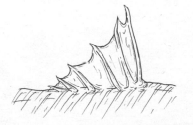

HAWAIIAN CARNIVOROUS CATERPILLAR

Eupithecia

(you-pith-e-sha)

Just under an inch (2.5 cm) long, the green to brown Hawaiian carnivorous caterpillar blends into the leaves and plants where it hunts. Using its rear prolegs to hold on to branches or leaves, the caterpillar waits. Sensitive hairs along its abdomen let it know when prey is near. The caterpillar then snaps forward, using its front claws to grab its meal—like something out of a horror movie!

Danger Factor

Although not a risk to humans, this small caterpillar is a serious threat to other insects. Scientists believe that it evolved to eat insects rather than flowers and seeds because the Hawaiian Islands didn't have typical insect predators, such as the praying mantis, when these islands first formed. Lucky for us, this caterpillar will never evolve to human-eating size (we hope).

What They Eat

With a strike so fast you need a slow-motion camera to see it, the Hawaiian carnivorous caterpillar is an incredible predator for its size. Its victims include flies, crickets, moths, cockroaches, and termites.

Conservation Status

NOT EVALUATED

Scientists do not know much about the population size or range of the carnivorous caterpillar. This is most likely due to how small they are, how well they camouflage, and the fact that they are found only on the Hawaiian Islands. But it is still important to protect this species, as it does an important job of keeping the ecosystem healthy by controlling the insect population.

Where They Live

Eupithecia caterpillars live all over the world, but the carnivorous species lives only on the Hawaiian Islands. These insect hunters are in the caterpillar stage for about 4 weeks. During this stage, they spend most of their time in trees and shrubs. When it is time to enter the pupa stage, they make a protective hole in the earth to spin a cocoon.

FUN FACTS

◆ The carnivorous caterpillar has the nicknames "inchworm" and "looper" because of the way it moves.

◆ When these caterpillars turn into moths, they're no longer carnivores.

◆ Masters of disguise! The carnivorous caterpillar is able to hide among sticks and leaves because it blends in and looks like a plant.

HOODED PITOHUI

Pitohui dichrous

(pit-o-hoo-ee die-cr-ow-s)

At 9 inches (22 cm) long from its head to its tail feathers, the hooded pitohui scans the forest with its dark, sometimes red, eyes. Puffing out its orange-feathered chest, it opens its strong black beak and whistles. As well as having a nasty smell, those brightly colored feathers let others know this bird's secret. Can you guess what it is? If you guessed that the hooded pitohui is poisonous, you're right! It's the most poisonous bird in the world.

Danger Factor

The hooded pitohui actually has the same toxin as the golden poison frog (page 58). Scientists believe this is because it eats a species of beetle from the same family as the beetle that gives the golden poison frog its toxin. They also think that the hooded pitohui uses this poison as a defense against predators and to protect it from parasites. Don't touch their pretty feathers, as the toxin causes a tingling, burning, and numbing sensation in humans.

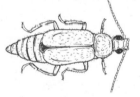

Conservation Status

LEAST CONCERN

The hooded pitohui's population is abundant on its native island. Since it lives in forests, its habitat could be affected by industries like logging, mining, and farming. But some researchers discovered that its population has actually increased in high mountain areas, despite disturbances to its habitat.

What They Eat

Hooded pitohuis gather with small groups of different bird species to forage on the forest floor and in the tree canopy. Fruit is a large part of its diet. It also seeks out insects, especially the poisonous beetle that makes it toxic and that is essential to its protection against predators.

Where They Live

The hooded pitohui can be found only on an island in the Pacific Ocean called New Guinea. This island has the warmer climate, tropical rain forest, and jungles that the bird loves and needs to make its home.

FUN FACTS

◆ Over a long period of time, some nonpoisonous birds started to look like the hooded pitohui. In biology, this evolution is called "mimicry." Predators think that the other birds are also poisonous and leave them alone.

◆ Some people still eat this bird, but it must be carefully prepared in order to remove all toxin-producing parts.

◆ Don't eat too many or you'll get a tummy ache! Scientists believe that, at first, hooded pitohuis ate only a few poisonous beetles at a time. They needed to build up a resistance to the poison over many years, or else eating the beetles would have killed them.

HUMAN BOTFLY

Dermatobia hominis

(derma-toby-a hom-in-is)

L ike a caterpillar, the human botfly starts its
life as a larva. When it emerges from its
chrysalis, it is a hairy flying insect with a
bright blue abdomen and huge red eyes. It grows to
be only about one half to three quarters of an inch
(1 to 2 cm) in size and is often compared to a
bumblebee. However, the parasitic human botfly
is much more dangerous.

Danger Factor

Female human botflies attach their eggs to a biting insect, such as a mosquito or tick. This insect then leaves the eggs on a "host," often a cow or dog but sometimes a human. The larvae hatch and then dig into their host, eating its flesh. This infestation is called "myiasis" and it is the reason why the human botfly is so dangerous. The larvae will continue to live within this safe environment for 1 to 2 months, until they arc ready to emerge as maggots. The best thing to do if you have a botfly larva inside your skin is either to leave it until it is ready to emerge naturally or block off its air supply by covering the area and patiently wait for it to die.

Conservation Status

NOT EVALUATED

Human botflies are considered quite a nuisance for both humans and animals because these parasites can infest a host with thousands of larvae at one time. Parasites are living organisms that use a host for food and shelter and give nothing in return, so you might think that their survival is not important. But until researchers fully understand the role that parasites, including the human botfly, play in the global ecosystem, we shouldn't try to destroy them.

What They Eat

The adult human botfly doesn't have any mouthparts. That's because it never eats! As a larva, it eats enough of its host's flesh to give it the energy it needs for its metamorphosis and short adulthood, which lasts just a few days. The larvae mostly feast on cows and dogs, they but also enjoy a livestock buffet of sheep, goats, and pigs.

Where They Live

Human botflies mostly live in South and Central America, but they occasionally hitch a ride elsewhere on a tourist returning home from a trip. Commercial farms with lots of tasty cattle in humid tropical and semitropical forests provide the perfect home for them.

FUN FACTS

◆ The first step to killing a human botfly larva that has burrowed into skin is to cover the wound and cut off its oxygen. To do this, people have used beeswax, petroleum jelly, duct tape, and even bacon. A traditional method uses the sap of the matatorsalo tree.

◆ Very considerate houseguests, human botfly larvae produce a painkilling substance so that their host feels as little as possible while they are feeding.

◆ These flies can lay up to 1,000 eggs.

INDIAN RED SCORPION

Hottentotta tamulus

(hot-ten-tota tam-u-lus)

At only 3.5 inches (almost 9 cm), the Indian red scorpion is an arachnid, meaning that it is in the same family as spiders. Ranging in body color from a bright red-orange to a dull brown, it has small pincers at its front and a large venom-filled stinger at its end. You can see its similarity to a spider in its eight legs and two body segments. Spiders and scorpions are two of the animals most feared by humans, and the Indian red scorpion, thought to be the world's deadliest scorpion, is especially scary.

Danger Factor

Despite its small size, the Indian red scorpion can really pack a wallop with its sting. If a person accidentally steps on one, they could die. But you can't really blame the scorpion. Its sting is its defense system, which it uses when it feels threatened, and even a child's foot would look pretty large and threatening to a scorpion! Its venom can cause vomiting, increased heart rate, and difficulty breathing.

Conservation Status

NOT EVALUATED

Not much is known about the population size or conservation status of the Indian red scorpion. Many species of birds snack on them and, despite their painful sting, humans keep them as pets. Their population size in the wild seems to be stable, but conservationists do not have an accurate count of their number.

What They Eat

This carnivorous creature hunts in the dark and relies on vibrations to sense prey, jumping onto critters like insects and lizards. Using its front pincers, it grabs its meal. If the prey is big, the scorpion may also use its stinger to paralyze its struggling victim. Then it sprays enzymes (or stomach acid) onto its catch. This turns the prey's body parts into a liquid that the scorpion sucks up. Can you imagine doing this three times a day? Luckily, the Indian red scorpion doesn't need to eat as often as you do. It can go weeks between feedings.

Where They Live

Like its name suggests, the Indian red scorpion lives in India. It also lives in Nepal, Pakistan, and Sri Lanka. Unlike its scorpion cousins who live in deserts, it prefers humid and tropical environments, though it avoids sunlight and hides in dark, rocky places during the day.

FUN FACTS

◆ Researchers use ultraviolet black lights to hunt for Indian red scorpions at night because this light turns them a fluorescent blue-green! Scientists think their exoskeleton has a natural ultraviolet coating that not only protects them from the sun but also makes them glow in the dark.

◆ Baby scorpions, called "scorplings," ride around on their mom's back until they shed their skin for the first time, about two weeks after their birth.

◆ Can I have this dance? When looking for a mate, a male scorpion grabs on to a female's pincers and leads her on a choreographed walk, called a "promenade à deux."

IRUKANDJI JELLYFISH

Carukia barnesi
(car-oo-kia bar-nes-ee)

I t's almost impossible to see the Irukandji jellyfish swimming in the ocean. Completely colorless, this invertebrate is an invisible danger.

Danger Factor

Irukandji jellyfish are incredibly dangerous, and their sting sends 50 to 100 people to the hospital every year. Its sting just feels like a mosquito bite at first. But it soon causes a person to feel excruciating pain throughout their body, as well as nausea, headache, and a racing heartbeat. These symptoms even have their own syndrome named after them, the Irukandji syndrome.

What They Eat

This daytime hunter actively searches for fish, shrimp, and other marine invertebrates. When it senses nearby prey, it extends a tentacle and twitches the end. The prey is attracted to the tentacle, but when it tries to take a bite, it gets a nasty surprise—a mouthful of venom! The jellyfish then uses the tentacle to reel the immobilized prey into its mouth and eats it.

Conservation Status

NOT EVALUATED

Because of the Irukandji jellyfish's small size and the vastness of its habitat, it is very difficult for scientists to study or even count them. But rising ocean temperatures and dying coral reefs negatively affect the habitat conditions of all marine life, including the Irukandji jellyfish.

Where They Live

This small but deadly jellyfish is mostly found in warm, shallow salt water along the northern Australian coastline. Scientists have spotted adult Irukandji jellyfish in deeper waters around the Great Barrier Reef.

FUN FACTS

◆ The Irukandji jellyfish does have eyes but manages to live without a brain! Rather than using one central command center, it uses a system of sensitive nerves just below the outer layer of its skin. Each part of this system sends signals for an individual action, such as swimming, eating, or stinging.

◆ No antivenom has been found for this jellyfish species.

◆ So little is known about the Irukandji jellyfish that we're not even certain how long they can live.

KISSING BUG

Triatoma dimidiata

(try-a-toe-ma dim-e-dee-ata)

This blood-sucking parasite is just one of over 130 kissing bug species. Its body is mostly black, with orange, brown, and yellow markings on its flat, oval back. Only about 1 inch (2.5 cm) long, it has a very long cone-shaped nose at the end of its sticklike head that pierces the skin of its prey. The kissing bug silently and gently feeds on, or "kisses," the skin around a sleeping person's eyes and mouth, sucking their blood. Usually, these love bites don't hurt, though they can leave red marks, and a person who is allergic to these insects' kisses might experience difficulty breathing.

Danger Factor

If you could open a kissing bug, you might find another, smaller parasite inside! This smaller parasite carries Chagas disease, which the kissing bug can unknowingly transfer to the blood of its prey. Chagas disease causes fever, headaches, and swollen lymph nodes. If left untreated over many years, Chagas disease can lead to much more serious symptoms and possibly death. Thankfully, not all kissing bugs carry this dangerous disease!

Where They Live

The *Triatoma dimidiata* species of the kissing bug lives in the rain forests of South and Central America and in southern Mexico. They are attracted to warmth and light, but tend to hide in rock piles or tree hollows.

Conservation Status

NOT EVALUATED

Kissing bug predators include lizards, rats, chickens, and toads, and there are also species of spiders and wasps that eat young kissing bugs. Even though they don't always spread Chagas disease to humans, there are efforts by health officials to reduce their numbers. But so far, most extermination methods have been unsuccessful, and, in fact, their population is growing. Researchers believe that deforestation and climate change are responsible for the rising number of kissing bugs.

What They Eat

As a nighttime feeder, a kissing bug usually waits for its human victim to fall asleep, as it is easier to feed that way. The bug goes in for a "kiss," piercing the skin and injecting a numbing protein that makes its bite painless. It then inserts its straw-shaped snout and starts sucking blood. It also gives kisses to warm-blooded animals that live near humans, such as dogs, cats, mice, chickens, and cattle.

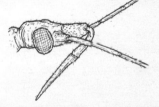

FUN FACTS

◆ In 1835, the famous scientist Charles Darwin wrote about kissing bugs in his journal. Darwin suffered from a mysterious illness for most of his adult life, and doctors now believe it might have been Chagas disease.

◆ Several insects found in the US resemble the kissing bug but are not harmful. Box-elder bugs and stink bugs are the most common.

◆ "Give mummy a good-night kiss!" The oldest mummies in the world, which were found in the Chilean desert and date back 9,000 years, contain traces of Chagas disease.

0.9–1.2 inches (25–30 mm)

KOMODO DRAGON

Varanus komodoensis

(var-a-nus komo-do-en-sis)

The Komodo dragon is the world's largest lizard, averaging 8 feet (2.5 m) in length and 170 pounds (77 kg) in weight. Resembling a mythical dragon, it is covered in scales, with a protective suit of armor called "osteoderm" (or bone) underneath. As a Komodo dragon gets older—some live for 50 years in the wild—its osteoderm becomes harder and stronger. Its tail is as long as its body, and its four beefy legs end in deadly claws. As if this didn't make it scary enough, the Komodo dragon has 60 serrated teeth that look like a saw and can rip prey apart very quickly.

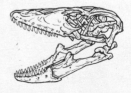

Danger Factor

The Komodo dragon is an extremely powerful apex predator, capable of tearing the throats of deer, goats, pigs, and even water buffalo. It is also very, very patient. If it cannot subdue a victim right away, it will stalk the wounded animal for hours, sometimes even days, until its prey eventually dies from the venom in the dragon's bite. Humans have occasionally been attacked, but only five people have been killed by a Komodo dragon.

Conservation Status

VULNERABLE

While these creatures have few natural predators, humans have encroached on their native habitat. But in 1980, Indonesia established Komodo National Park to help protect the dragons from hunters and poachers and to provide conservation education to the local islanders.

What They Eat

Komodo dragons eat just about anything with four legs, from pigs and deer to water buffalo and horses. They hunt their own prey, but they are also scavengers that eat carrion, or the leftovers of another animal's kill. Komodo dragons can eat a lot in one sitting—up to 80 percent of their body weight. And they metabolize, or burn energy, very slowly, which means that they can survive on as few as 12 good meals per year.

Where They Live

Komodo dragons are found on only 5 of Indonesia's 17,000 islands. Young Komodo dragons spend the first few months of their lives up in the trees of the tropical forests in order to stay safe from predators. Adults spend their days resting in the shade. At night, these cold-blooded creatures sleep alone in small burrows, which helps them conserve body heat and stay warm.

FUN FACTS

◆ Komodo dragons use their long, forked tongues to taste the air and can recognize scents up to 5 miles (8 km) away!

◆ Scientists believe that Komodo dragons first lived In Australia millions of years ago. They suspect that the dragons walked from Australia to Indonesia when the sea levels were drastically lowered during the last ice age.

◆ The largest of the world's largest lizards is on record as reaching a whopping 10.3 feet (3.1 m) and 366 pounds (166 kg)!

LEOPARD SEAL

Hydrurga leptonyx

(hi-drurg-a lep-ton-ix)

Despite reaching lengths of 11.5 feet (3.5 m) and weights of 1,000 pounds (450 kg), the massive leopard seal darts through the Antarctic waters at impressive speeds, while also playfully twisting and flipping. It has large front flippers, each with webbed digits, and its fur is covered with dark "leopard" spots. Its enormous upturned mouth is full of sharp canine teeth. The second-largest species of seal in Antarctica, the leopard seal is designed for survival.

Danger Factor

The leopard seal uses its large, powerful teeth to tear apart its prey and, like a cat, often plays with its catch before eating it. These elusive seals usually regard the few divers, photographers, and scientists they encounter with curiosity and playfulness. Attacks on humans are infrequent, but in 2003, a leopard seal did kill a British scientist, though it is unclear whether it was an accident or on purpose.

Conservation Status

LEAST CONCERN

Although the leopard seal's population is currently large and stable, climate change is an impending threat. Sheets of polar pack ice provide the seals with a place to come out of the water, have a snack, and maybe take a nap. Female leopard seals give birth on the ice. The pack ice in Antarctica is melting, which means less room for these important parts of a leopard seal's life.

What They Eat

Gulp! Leopard seals love to eat krill, a small crustacean similar to shrimp. They also feast on squid, fish, penguins, birds, and even other seals. Their powerful jaws and teeth help them quickly devour any meal.

Where They Live

Leopard seals live in the southern hemisphere, in the south polar waters of the Antarctic region and slightly north around the sub-Antarctic islands. They spend most of their day in the water and can stay underwater for 15 to 30 minutes. They are skilled swimmers and divers, and one seal was even recorded at a depth of almost 1,000 feet (304 m).

FUN FACTS

◆ Considered an apex predator in Antarctica, the leopard seal's only potential threat is the orca, or killer whale.

◆ Big babies! Leopard seal pups can weigh 66 to 77 pounds (30 to 35 kg) and measure more than 5 feet (1.6 m) when they're born.

◆ The whiskers of the leopard seal are so sensitive that, even in murky water, they can sense which fish are largest, helping them find the worthiest pursuit.

MOOSE

Alces americanus

(al-ces am-eri-can-us)

An enormous member of the deer family, the moose is not an animal you could easily miss! It averages 9 feet (2.7 m) tall and can weigh as much as 900 pounds (408 kg). An adult male's rack of antlers can be 6 feet (1.8 m) wide from tip to tip and weigh close to 50 pounds (22 kg). Covered in thick brown fur, this hoofed beast has a large nose, rotating ears, and a humped back. A long piece of loose skin, called a "dewlap" or "bell," dangles from its chin. They rely on their sharp hooves to kick anything that poses a threat (but do this mostly to protect their calves).

Danger Factor

Have you ever been so hungry that you got mad? Or so tired that you got grumpy? Well, guess what? That can happen to animals, too. Moose become aggressive when food is scarce, during the mating season, and when protecting their young. They'll stomp their feet, charge forward, and kick at a person. In Alaska alone, 5 to 10 people are injured by moose each year. Wildlife experts recommend always keeping your distance.

Conservation Status

LEAST CONCERN

Moose live all over the world and are abundant throughout their ever-growing range. Young moose are prey to brown bears and wolves, and people hunt moose for food and sport. Despite this, the population of the *Alces americanus* species of moose is increasing in some northeastern parts of the United States and in Canada. Protecting forests helps protect moose.

What They Eat

The moose is an herbivore and loves twigs, bark, roots, and willow tree shoots. Because of their huge size, moose must eat 9,770 calories a day, and they can eat up to 70.5 pounds (almost 32 kg) of food each day. They probably spend most of their day either eating or thinking about eating!

Where They Live

If you look closely at its species name, you can probably guess where the *Alces americanus* lives. They roam the forests, woodlands, and lowland mountains of North America, from Canada and Alaska into the northeastern United States and as far south as the Rocky Mountains in Colorado. Summers can get a little hot for them, so they need freshwater streams and lakes nearby.

FUN FACTS

◆ The word "moose" comes from the Algonquin Indian word "moosewa," which means "eater of twigs."

◆ Male moose shed their antlers in late fall and start growing a new set in the spring. Losing their antlers helps them conserve energy and stay warm over the winter.

◆ Moose are excellent swimmers. They can swim up to 6 miles (9 km) per hour, while most humans can swim only 2 miles (3 km) per hour. And they can't drown because their thick fur coats and hollow hair act like a life jacket!

MOSAIC CRAB

Lophozozymus pictor

(lof-o-zoz-eye-mus pic-tor)

An artist makes a mosaic by arranging small pieces of stones, shells, and glass into patterns and pictures. The mosaic reef crab gets its name from the beautiful mosaic-like patterns found on its wide back shell. As the crab grows, it will molt, or shed, its shell, but each new shell still has the same mosaic pattern. With eight hairy walking legs and two short black-tipped claws, or pincers, at the front, this 3.5-inch (8.8 cm) crustacean scuttles sideways.

Danger Factor

This small crab contains two deadly neurotoxins that are so powerful they can paralyze and even kill a human. Just like the golden poison frog on page 58 and the hooded pitohui on page 68, the mosaic reef crab gets its toxins from something it eats: a poisonous sea cucumber. The toxins slowly multiply in the crab's body, and there's no way to remove the poison from the crabmeat, making it dangerous for anything unfortunate enough to eat it.

Conservation Status

NOT EVALUATED

The Republic of Singapore, one of the countries where the mosaic reef crab lives, considers the animal to be endangered. Habitat loss from polluted oceans and dying coral reefs is partly to blame.

What They Eat

Crunch! The mosaic reef crab eats a variety of sea vegetation, such as the poisonous sea cucumber. It also cracks into meatier options like sea urchins, clams, and sea stars, as well as fish, sea worms, barnacles, marine plants, and more.

Where They Live

These crabs can be viewed among the rocky shores and coral rubble of the Indo-Pacific region, including in Australian waters and around islands such as Singapore. It likes to hang out in water up to 16 feet (5 m) deep.

FUN FACTS

◆ Their toxin, known as "saxitoxin," is 1,000 times deadlier than cyanide. In captivity, mosaic reef crabs lose their toxicity within a month, which supports scientists' belief that they get their poison through their diet.

◆ The mosaic reef crab's scientific name, *Pictor*, translates to "painter" in Latin.

◆ Can you see a similarity in coloring between the mosaic reef crab and the geography cone snail on page 50? The striking colors and patterns of both these creatures warn predators that they are not safe to eat. This trait is called "aposematism."

◆ Crabs can move forward but are much faster when they move sideways.

ORIENTAL RAT FLEA

Xenopsylla cheopis
(zen-op-sill-a chee-o-pee)

*T*hey want to suck your blood! Barely visible at an average size of a hundredth of an inch (2.5 mm), the dark reddish-brown, wingless oriental rat flea—named after the source of its favorite meal—lives on nothing but blood for its short life. It relies on its very powerful three pairs of legs to travel. Thanks to a special protein in its body, this tiny gymnast stores up energy and releases it all in one acrobatic move—an almost 12-inch (30 cm) jump that turns into a backflip! In this way, it leaps from nest to nest and victim to victim.

Conservation Status

NOT EVALUATED

Because the oriental rat flea is a parasite, conservationists are concerned with limiting the flea's population and range. As the planet's temperature rises, the oriental rat flea will be able to survive in more parts of the world.

What They Eat

Rat blood is the most popular meal for the oriental rat flea, but any mammal's blood will do, including a human's.

Where They Live

Found worldwide, in tropical and temperate climates, the oriental rat flea likes both the country and the city. Anywhere with a warm climate and a high population of rats can be home to the oriental rat flea. It lives in its hosts' nests, including human beds. Sewers, underground tunnels, and seaports are some of its favorite urban hangouts.

Danger Factor

If a flea sucks the blood of a rat that is sick, the infected blood can then be transferred to the next person or animal the flea bites, making that victim sick, too. The worst time this happened was in the 14th century, when the oriental flea spread a disease called the bubonic plague all over Asia and Europe, killing approximately 50 million people. Adult oriental fleas can live up to a year, giving them plenty of time to spread illness far and wide.

FUN FACTS

◆ Oriental rat fleas can jump up to 200 times their body length. But they can't control which direction they go in and must land wherever their leap takes them.

◆ During the bubonic plague, doctors believed the disease was spread through bad smells, so they wore masks to protect themselves. The masks had large beaks stuffed with good-smelling herbs, to fight the bad smells and prevent them from getting sick.

◆ Discovered in Egypt in 1903, these fleas were named *Xenopsylla cheopis* for the Pharaoh Cheops, who built the Great Pyramid at Giza.

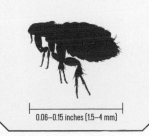

0.06–0.15 inches (1.5–4 mm)

OSTRICH

Struthio camelus

(struth-eye-o camel-us)

Did you know that not all birds can fly? A group of birds called "ratites" have feathers but cannot fly, and the ostrich belongs to this group. It makes up for not flying by being the fastest two-legged animal in the world, able to run up to 40 miles (64 km) per hour and using its short wings to steer rather than soar. Ostriches are also the tallest birds, averaging 6 to 9 feet (1.8 to 2.7 m), and the heaviest, weighing from 140 to 320 pounds (58 to 145 kg).

Danger Factor

Hiss! That's how an ostrich lets you know to stay away. Even though its first instinct is to run from danger, it will attack a threat to its eggs or itself. Its powerful legs aren't just for running. Each foot has a 4-inch-long (10 cm) claw that is capable of slicing open (and killing) lions, cheetahs, leopards, and even humans.

Conservation Status

LEAST CONCERN

In the 18th century, ostriches almost became extinct because people wanted to wear their beautiful feathers. While ostrich farms have helped to preserve the range and population of ostriches in the wild, their numbers are still decreasing. Some subspecies have become extinct or endangered because of hunting and habitat loss.

What They Eat

Although ostriches are primarily herbivores and usually picky eaters, choosing particular seeds from flowers and grasses, they will finish their meat-eating neighbors' leftovers. They can go for days without drinking water. Instead, they pull moisture from the plants they eat. But they must consume around 8 pounds (3.5 kg) of food per day for energy.

Where They Live

Once found throughout a very wide range, wild ostriches now live only in central and southern Africa. In the past, their range extended to the Arabian Peninsula and southwestern Asia, but they were hunted to near extinction there.

FUN FACTS

◆ My, what big eyes you have! An ostrich's eye is larger than its brain. Its brain weighs about 1.4 ounces (40 g) but one of its eyes weighs 2 ounces (56.5 g)!

◆ You might have heard that ostriches bury their heads in the sand, but this is actually a myth. They do lie with their heads pressed down flat to the ground when they feel threatened. It looks like the ostrich has buried its head because the color of its head and neck blend in with the color of the sand.

◆ The size of an ostrich egg is equal to approximately 24 chicken eggs.

PORK TAPEWORM

Taenia solium

(tee-nee-uh sole-ee-um)

A flat, ribbonlike parasite that grows to lengths of 6 to 9 feet (1.8 to 2.6 m) and sometimes longer, the pork tapeworm lives in the small intestines of pigs and humans. If a pig eats food that has tapeworm eggs in it, those eggs hatch in the pig's intestine. Tiny tapeworm larvae can then be transferred to a person who eats undercooked pork. These uninvited guests use their four front-end suckers and tiny body hooks to attach to their host's intestine.

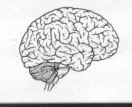

Danger Factor

Most people who consume a pork tapeworm experience only mild symptoms, like a stomachache. Doctors can prescribe medicine to kill a tapeworm, and cooking pork thoroughly to kill any larvae is an important step toward preventing this parasite from living inside you. The real danger is if a person ingests the eggs before they hatch. This can happen by eating food, drinking water, or accidentally ingesting droppings that have tapeworm eggs in it. The larvae from those eggs can enter your bloodstream and travel to different organs. If they reach the brain, they can cause a very dangerous disease called neurocysticercosis, which can cause eye and muscle damage, seizures, and potentially death.

Conservation Status

NOT EVALUATED

The pork tapeworm is mostly considered a nuisance, and its conservation status has not been evaluated. In fact, many researchers are trying to find ways to control its population. Scientists are studying a vaccine for pigs that would disrupt the pork tapeworm's life cycle.

What They Eat

Unlike other parasites, the pork tapeworm has no mouth or stomach. Instead, it absorbs nutrients from the intestinal walls of its host directly into its body segments. The small intestine breaks down food after it passes through the stomach, so that the body absorbs needed nutrients, such as vitamins, minerals, proteins, carbohydrates, and fats. There's no better place for a nutrition-stealing tapeworm to be.

Where They Live

Wherever pigs live, pork tapeworms live! They can be found especially in places where uncooked meat is eaten and in countries where clean drinking water is not always available.

FUN FACTS

◆ Pork tapeworms can live undetected in an intestine for 5 to 25 years.

◆ The segments of a tapeworm are called "proglottids," and an adult pork tapeworm can have as many as 1,000!

◆ This species is very different from the tapeworms found in dogs and cats. Our pets usually contract their tapeworms from fleas that carry tapeworm larvae.

RED-BELLIED PIRANHA

Pygocentrus nattereri

(pie-go-cen-trus nat-er-air-ee)

Piranhas have a bad reputation, and in popular culture they are often portrayed as being out to get us. While they are dangerous and can be aggressive, it is not for the reasons that some might believe. In reality, piranhas swarm only when the water is low, food is scarce, or they feel threatened. They grow to around 1 foot (30 cm) long and can weigh 8 pounds (3.5 kg). Their powerful jaws are packed with razor-sharp teeth.

Danger Factor

Because of the piranhas' ability to swarm, their flesh-tearing teeth, and their ferocity during feeding, they are considered dangerous. The red-bellied piranha can bite chunks out of the flesh of other river dwellers, and humans will often suffer bites to their hands and feet. Studies suggest that loud noises, splashing about, and emptying fish contents into the water you are swimming in are some of the key factors linked to piranha attacks. Scientists believe that in most cases of reported deaths the victim was already dead when the fish decided to snack on the body. Piranhas do not attack people who simply enter the water. However, they can cause serious damage under certain circumstances and should be treated with respect and caution.

Conservation Status

NOT EVALUATED

The red-bellied piranha's conservation status has not yet been evaluated. It has been introduced to a range of new locations over the years, most likely by accident, and is usually killed by government agencies.

What They Eat

A common misconception is that piranhas only feed by swarming on large mammals. They actually rely on a range of food sources, including aquatic invertebrates, insects, fish, and even plants. Some piranha species are totally herbivorous!

Where They Live

Found in South America, the red-bellied piranha resides in lakes and rivers in the Amazon and Paraná-Paraguay basins, as well as parts of northeast Brazil.

FUN FACTS

◆ Former US president Theodore Roosevelt came across the piranha in 1913 while traveling around South America. In his book *Through the Brazilian Wilderness*, he wrote: 'They will devour alive any wounded man or beast; for blood in the water excites them to madness.' This comment is one reason why piranhas got such a bad reputation.

◆ Part of their mating display includes swimming around in circles.

◆ Piranhas can smell a single drop of blood in 53 gallons (200 L) of water.

◆ When pursuing its prey, the piranha will go for the eyes and tail, in order to make sure its victim cannot get away.

RED-HEADED MOUSE SPIDER

Missulena occatoria

(miss-you-lee-na oc-ca-tor-ia)

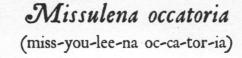

L arge and stout, with short legs, female red-headed mouse spiders are approximately twice the size of males, reaching 1.3 inches (3.3 cm), and have a black abdomen with a red tinge. The males grow to about three fifths of an inch (1.5 cm) and have long legs, a blue-black abdomen, a bright red head, and red jaws.

Danger Factor

Red-headed mouse spiders contain a venom toxic enough to kill a human, although this is very uncommon. The spider is not usually aggressive, and it more often gives a "dry" bite when startled or threatened, meaning it does not inject venom. This allows it to save its small reserve of venom for serious threats.

Conservation Status

NOT EVALUATED

The red-headed mouse spider spends most of its life in an underground burrow, which makes it difficult for scientists to count its population. Its predators include scorpions, centipedes, bandicoots, and even parasitic wasps.

What They Eat

This spider sets silk trip lines. When prey triggers a trip line, the spider lunges through the opening of its burrow and then drags its meal inside. Its diet consists mostly of insects and other spiders, but it will also eat small vertebrates, like lizards and frogs.

Where They Live

Baby spiders climb high and release silk threads that catch the wind (known as "ballooning"), sending them to new homes. Scientists believe this is why the red-headed mouse spider has spread so far across mainland Australia. Once it lands in forest or shrubland, it builds a large, silk-covered burrow that can be as deep as 20 inches (55 cm).

FUN FACTS

◆ These spiders have the word "mouse" in their name because scientists first thought that their burrows were the same as mouse burrows.

◆ Male and female red-headed mouse spiders look so different that scientists used to think they were two separate species.

◆ Ancient groups of spiders moved their fangs straight up and down, but modern spiders, like the red-headed mouse spider, move their jaws in and out from side to side.

RED DEVIL SQUID

Dosidicus gigas

(doe-sid-e-cus gi-gas)

Its common name is Humboldt squid, but fearful fishers call this jumbo flying squid "diablo roja," Spanish for "red devil." The largest member of the flying squid family, its mantle (the top part of its body) can be close to 5 feet (1.5 m) long and, including its eight arms and two tentacles, it can weigh close to 100 pounds (45 kg). Each tentacle has between 100 and 200 suckers on it, which are useful for catching prey—and perhaps the occasional fisher.

Danger Factor

Legend has it that the red devil squid will drag humans into the water and rip them apart in minutes. Some biologists believe this is an exaggeration. But a red devil squid is a powerful creature, and if you are unlucky enough to be in the water with one, you might very well be in danger. Like many animals, it attacks when it is hungry or scared.

Conservation Status

DATA DEFICIENT

Because it prefers to stay deep in the ocean, there is no official count of the population of the red devil squid. But it is the most heavily fished cephalopod by commercial fishers, and continued fishing could ultimately harm its population. Its natural predators include sperm whales, striped marlin, and deep-sea sharks.

What They Eat

Propelling itself quickly through the water, the red devil squid pursues its prey. The suckers on its arms work like tiny sharp teeth, hooking fish, crustaceans, and smaller squid, which it then pulls into its sharp, beak-like mouth.

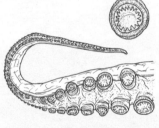

Where They Live

The red devil squid mostly lives in the eastern Pacific Ocean, from northern California to southern Chile. Recently, some have been spotted as far north as Canada. The red devil squid hangs out anywhere from just beneath the surface of the water to 3,300 feet (1,000 m) deep.

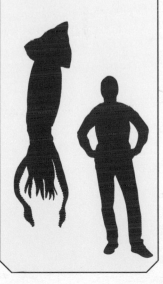

RED KANGAROO

Macropus rufus

(macro-pus ru-fuss)

The largest marsupial in the world, a male red kangaroo has a body length of 3 to 4 feet (90 to 120 cm), with 3 to 4 feet of tail, and a female's body length is 2 to 3 feet (60 to 90 cm), with a 2-foot tail. Tendons in their muscular hind legs stretch and contract like rubber bands, powering jumps 6 feet (1.8 m) high and up to 25 feet (7.5 m) long. A red kangaroo can use its short forelegs, along with its tail, to walk. But hopping is much more fun!

Danger Factor

Kangaroos are known for "boxing" when they fight, hitting out with their forepaws and kicking with their large, strong feet. The stronger kicks of a red kangaroo have the potential to disembowel a victim. Most fights between kangaroos are between males competing with each another for dominance and mating rights. Attacks on humans are rare but can happen if a kangaroo is startled or feels threatened.

Conservation Status

LEAST CONCERN

Dingoes and wild dogs will occasionally kill adult kangaroos, but they usually prey on joeys, or newborns. Ranchers and farmers consider kangaroos a pest and sometimes shoot them. Nevertheless, the population of red kangaroos is stable, and it is important to keep them safe as they play a crucial role in managing the vegetation of their environment.

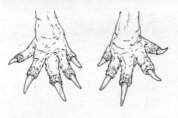

What They Eat

This kangaroo is an herbivore that always eats its greens. It grazes mostly on grasses, but pretty much any leafy green plant will do. Finding water in its native habitat can be difficult, so the red kangaroo eats moisture-filled succulent plants to keep hydrated.

Where They Live

Red kangaroos live primarily in central and western Australia. Found in several biomes, they thrive in dry and arid climates and sparsely wooded or open plain habitats. A group of kangaroos will escape the daytime heat by lying down under shady trees and bushes.

FUN FACTS

◆ Growing pains? Newborn joeys are only one tenth of an inch (2.5 cm) long!

◆ Besides jumping high, kangaroos can speed-hop up to 35 miles (56 km) per hour and swim short distances.

◆ Red kangaroos use their left forepaws for fine motor skills, such as eating and grooming, and their right for skills requiring strength.

RED LIONFISH

Pterois volitans

(tero-is voli-tans)

The mix of patterns and colors on the red lionfish lets other sea creatures know that it is deadly. This king of the ocean, barely more than a foot (30 cm) long, is loaded with toxins: 13 venomous spines line its back, with 3 more on its rear and another on each fin. Given that it has a 10- to 18-year life span and almost no natural predators, it seems everyone has gotten the message!

Danger Factor

The red lionfish has venom glands in every spine. A sting from these spines can cause terrible pain, nausea, seizures, limb paralysis, and even heart failure. Scientists estimate that up to 50,000 red lionfish stings happen each year.

Conservation Status

NOT EVALUATED

Red lionfish are considered invasive in many regions and drive away important native species that are vital to coral reefs. Their population is exploding outside their native waters. However, as with all marine life, these beautiful animals face some threats due to ocean pollution and its impact on their food sources.

What They Eat

Sunset is prime hunting time for the red lionfish. Blending in with the coral reef, it gulps down unsuspecting small fish, crustaceans, and marine invertebrates in one bite. It eats so quickly that the prey might not even notice it's been eaten until it's down the hatch!

Where They Live

These ocean invaders' native waters are off the coasts of Australia and throughout the Indo-Pacific region, including Malaysia, southern Korea, and southern Japan. Invasive populations can be found along the Atlantic coast, from North Carolina to Florida and the coasts of Bermuda, the Bahamas, and throughout the Caribbean. Rocky coastlines, coral reefs, and submerged shipwrecks provide the perfect nooks and crannies for hunting and hiding.

FUN FACTS

◆ Young lionfish have "wigglers," fleshy knobs over their eyes and under their mouth that attract smaller prey. As the fish becomes more experienced at hunting, these training tools disappear!

◆ Instead of swimming away when scared, the red lionfish will stay and point its spines at the threat.

◆ The same antivenom used for the red lionfish is believed to work against the sting of the reef stonefish (page 102).

REEF STONEFISH

Synanceia verrucosa
(sigh-nan-sea-a ver-ruh-co-sa)

It's easy to swim right past the reef stonefish as it hides on the shallow seafloor among the rocks and coral. With its camouflage of bumpy brown-and-gray skin, this foot-long (30 cm) fish blends in perfectly with its environment. But don't be fooled into thinking it's just another rock! With 13 fat, thumbtack-size, venom-filled spines along its dorsal fin, this fish is very dangerous.

Danger Factor

The reef stonefish may be the deadliest fish in the sea. Each of its 13 spines has 2 venom sacs. Its venom is a defense mechanism, released when the fish feels pressure, such as a footstep, on its body. A prick from one of these spines can cause excruciating pain, breathing issues, heart failure, and possible death. Experts advise wearing thick-soled shoes if you are in reef stonefish habitat.

Conservation Status

LEAST CONCERN

The reef stonefish's population is currently stable, and its preference for living in protected nooks and crannies means that it faces very few threats. But its continued survival depends on a healthy reef system.

What They Eat

Camouflaged and able to sit motionless for hours, the reef stonefish waits for small fish, shrimp, and other marine invertebrates to swim past its face, saving its energy for surprise attacks. As soon as a tasty morsel is near, it opens its mouth and sucks in its prey—lightning fast!

Where They Live

The reef stonefish lives in the shallow tropical saltwater reef systems throughout the Pacific and Indian Oceans, the Red Sea, and the east African coast.

FUN FACTS

◆ The reef stonefish can survive for up to 24 hours out of the water as long as it is surrounded by moist sand or rocks.

◆ Sharks and rays aren't fooled by the reef stonefish's disguise and will purposefully eat it.

◆ To protect yourself from getting stung by a venomous sea creature like the reef stonefish, slide your feet slowly through the sand as you walk into the water, rather than lifting your feet up and setting them down. This warns fish of your approach and means less pressure is applied if you accidentally bump into a reef stonefish!

◆ Although it's considered the most venomous fish in the world, in rare cases it has been sold for its meat in fish markets.

ROUGH-SKINNED NEWT

Taricha granulosa
(tar-e-ka gran-you-low-sa)

When threatened, the rough-skinned newt bends its head back and curls its tail, exposing its bright yellow-orange underside. Roughly 6 inches (15 cm) long, with four short legs and a long tail, this semiaquatic amphibian looks like a blend of a frog and a lizard. It gets its name from the dry, bumpy, brown skin on its top half. But this skin isn't as dull as it looks—it's covered in toxin.

Danger Factor

Rough-skinned newts release a milky neurotoxin through their skin. If you touch one, your skin might feel irritated. But since they are only poisonous if eaten, they are not a threat to people. Creatures that do not heed the rough-skinned newt's warning pose and eat it end up with the deadly toxin in their stomachs!

Conservation Status

LEAST CONCERN

Scientists estimate that there are over 100,000 rough-skinned newts in the wild, which means there is no immediate concern for their population. Like the gila monster (page 56), one of the dangers the newt faces is crossing a human-made road! So it is important to drive cautiously when close to their habitats.

What They Eat

Slurp! Rough-skinned newts slowly approach their prey and then quickly suck it into their mouth. If the prey is large, they grab it with their jaws and hold it in place with their teeth and tongue. Adult newts eat insects, arachnids, and worms.

Where They Live

Native to North America, rough-skinned newts live primarily on the West Coast, from central California to Alaska. Preferring temperate climates, they can be spotted in forest and mountain biomes with lakes and ponds. Adults in lower elevations spend cold days curled up in groups of 12 or more, tucked under logs and stones.

FUN FACTS

◆ A species of snake called the common garter snake is resistant to the rough-skinned newt's deadly toxin, making it one of the newt's very few predators.

◆ Males become smoother and lighter-colored during mating season. Females cover their eggs with toxin to protect them.

◆ What do a newt and an octopus have in common? The neurotoxin in the rough-skinned newt is the same one found in the southern blue-ringed octopus (page 110).

◆ Better than a mouse trap! One rough-skinned newt has enough poison to kill 25,000 mice.

SHORTFIN MAKO SHARK

Isurus oxyrinchus

(eye-sur-us oxy-rin-cuss)

*T*he fastest shark in the world, the shortfin mako shark is capable of hitting 43 miles (70 km) per hour while pursuing other fish. Quite impressive for a fish that averages 10 feet (3 m) in length and can weigh up to 300 pounds (135 kg)!

Short side fins and a vertical crescent tail help it glide silently through deep open water. Its large, triangular, extremely sharp teeth are visible even when its mouth is closed. No wonder scuba divers fear this shark's approach!

Danger Factor

While the shortfin mako shark is often accused of attacking humans, according to the International Shark Attack File, there have been only nine confirmed unprovoked attacks, with one fatality, since 1958. The shortfin mako shark also has a reputation for being dangerous outside its habitat. If it is dragged into a boat on a fishing line, it thrashes around to try to free itself, sometimes biting or crushing anyone unlucky enough to get in its way.

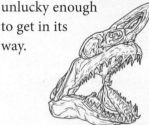

Conservation Status

ENDANGERED

Humans are the shortfin mako shark's only predator, but that's enough to make it endangered. These sharks are caught commercially for their meat, fins, liver, and oil. They are also popular among big-game recreational fishers. Although they are released back into the water, some sharks die not long after because of injuries or the stress of being caught.

What They Eat

These carnivores eat other sea creatures, such as fish, octopuses, squid, dolphins, and turtles, but bluefish are their favorite.

Where They Live

Shortfin makos will travel long distances in search of the perfect meal or mate. They live throughout the Pacific, Atlantic, and Indian Oceans, as well as the Mediterranean and Red Seas. Usually found in open water, they swim between the surface and 1,600 feet (487 m) deep.

FUN FACTS

◆ Because they swim so fast, these sharks can leap as high as 15 to 20 feet (4.5 to 6 m) out of the water!

◆ Save some for later! Shortfin mako sharks will change their eating habits, switching prey if a supply gets low, to make sure they don't overhunt a particular food.

◆ The shortfin mako shark is very smart. Scientists discovered that it has one of the largest brain-to-body-ratios of all the sharks studied.

SIX-SPOT BURNET MOTH

Zygaena filipendulae
(zye-gee-nah fil-ip-en-dew-lay)

Sporting six vibrant red spots each, the wings of the six-spot burnet moth extend from its thorax and stretch approximately 1 to 2 inches (3 to 4 cm) across when opened. It lays yellow-orange eggs on the undersides of leaves, and bright greenish-yellow, black-dotted caterpillars emerge. It's the caterpillar's diet that makes the six-spot burnet moth dangerous.

Danger Factor

The six-spot burnet caterpillar eats the leaves of the bird's-foot trefoil plant, which contains toxins that the caterpillar metabolizes into a poison called hydrogen cyanide. The six-spot burnet moth emerges from its cocoon containing the same toxin. Both caterpillar and moth are immune to the toxin, but their bird predators are not.

Conservation Status

NOT EVALUATED

The six-spot burnet moth is abundant throughout its range. However, these and other nectar-loving pollinators depend on undisturbed grassland biomes. Human activities can destroy the native wild plants necessary to its survival.

What They Eat

Adult six-spot burnet moths drink nectar from local wildflowers, such as flowering thistles, vetch, verbena, and knapweed. Pincushion flowers, a member of the honeysuckle family, are a particular favorite. This moth carries its own reusable drinking straw—its proboscis. Curled at the end of the moth's head, the straw unfurls when the moth is ready to drink.

Where They Live

The six-spot burnet moth is the most commonly spotted moth in Britain and the Republic of Ireland. They enjoy sand dunes, cliff edges, grasslands, and woodland habitats.

FUN FACTS

- Six-spot burnet moths have evolved to mimic the colors of the cinnabar moth, another poisonous species.

- Sometimes, the spots on these moths will blend together, making them look like another species of burnet moth whose wings have only five spots.

- That was a long nap! Some six-spot burnet caterpillars hibernate through two winters.

- These moths are often found in groups of several hundred.

- Swarm! The six-spot burnet moth likes to stay in large groups—often with several hundred individuals.

SOUTHERN BLUE-RINGED OCTOPUS

Hapalochlaena maculosa

(hap-al-o-clay-na mack-you-low-sa)

Measuring barely 8 inches (20 cm) from the top of its mantle to the end of an arm and weighing about 1 ounce (26 g), the yellowish-brown body of the southern blue-ringed octopus is camouflaged among the ocean rocks. But if this venomous cephalopod gets angry or frightened, it puts on a flashing light show. Sixty or more rings all over its body flash an electric blue, warning predators to stay away or else.

Danger Factor

When a southern blue-ringed octopus bites in self-defense, its small beak-like mouth transfers a powerful neurotoxin from its saliva into the wound. This bite is so gentle that a victim may not even know they have been bitten until they start feeling dizzy a few minutes later. They might then start to have trouble breathing and moving. There's no antivenom, and it takes about 24 hours for the toxin to leave a person's body, so without immediate medical attention, they could die.

Conservation Status

LEAST CONCERN

Southern blue ringed octopuses are sometimes captured for home aquariums, and human development along the coastline can affect their shallow-water habitats. But for now they are found over a wide area and have a large population.

What They Eat

The southern blue-ringed octopus relies on its toxin to hunt fish and crustaceans, including crabs, shellfish, and shrimp. It can release its venom into the water, paralyzing fish that absorb the toxin through their gills, or it can bite into a crustacean, injecting venom and killing it instantly.

Where They Live

Finding peace and quiet in the dark, the southern blue-ringed octopus squeezes into crevices, holes, and rocks in shallow reefs and tidal pools off the southern coast of Australia. Sometimes it will block the entrance to its hiding place with rocks and gravel, to protect itself from predators.

FUN FACTS

◆ The toxin is also found in blue-ringed octopus eggs, most likely to deter predators from feasting on their young.

◆ Blue-ringed octopuses are the only octopuses with enough venom to kill a person. In fact, one octopus has enough venom to kill 26 people.

◆ Octopuses release ink clouds as a self-defense mechanism, but the southern blue-ringed octopus lost its ability to produce ink. Scientists believe this may be because its toxin provides enough protection.

SPIDER-TAILED HORNED VIPER

Pseudocerastes urarachnoides

(sew-dos-er-ast-ees your-a-rack-noid-ees)

In 1970, scientists examined a dead snake with an unusual tail. They thought that the end of this horned viper's tail was simply a deformity or a tumor, until they found another snake with the same tail in 2003. In 2006, scientists officially recorded the spider-tailed horned viper as a new species. But is the thing at the end of its tail really a spider?

Danger Factor

It's not actually a mutated spider on this viper's tail. It's an evolutionary adaptation that acts as a fleshy lure to attract prey. The snake mimics the movements of a spider, wiggling its tail about and moving the "legs." When a bird comes close to peck at the "spider," the viper springs out and catches its meal. Its ability to imitate a different species makes this snake especially sneaky.

What They Eat

Using its lure, an adult spider-tailed horned viper attracts mostly migratory birds. The local birds seem to have caught onto its trick. But it still needs to act fast. If it is not quick enough, the bird might bite off the "spider"!

Conservation Status

DATA DEFICIENT

Because this species was first recorded very recently, there is little known about the population size of the spider-tailed horned viper and its conservation status. However, naturalists worry that it will soon face the same sorts of threats that other vipers do, such as being poached and illegally sold, locals killing it out of fear, and habitat destruction.

Where They Live

The spider-tailed horned viper lives in western Iran, in the hilly, arid Zagros Mountains. It is very difficult to spot because its color blends into the rocks where it lives. It hides in cracks and crevasses, leaving just its spiderlike tail exposed, to attract potential prey.

FUN FACTS

◆ The spider-tailed horned viper's lure starts to develop soon after the snake is born. In its youth, it practices hunting small lizards. Its "spider" is fully formed by the time the viper is an adult.

◆ Tricking prey by using a tail lure that looks like another animal is called "caudal luring" or "tail luring," and it is common among lizards, snakes, and even sharks. But according to some researchers, no species has a more elaborate lure than the spider-tailed horned viper.

◆ The spider-tailed horned viper has another advantage when hunting. Its pupils are slit-shaped in order to better see its prey before ambushing it.

◆ A group of vipers is called a "generation."

TASMANIAN DEVIL

Sarcophilus harrisii

(sar-coff-ilus harris-ee-eye)

When Europeans first moved to Australia and heard horrible growls, screeches, and shrieks, they thought the land was filled with demons. But these terrifying sounds came from a 2.5-foot (70 cm), 20-pound (9 kg) marsupial, which they named "devil." Tasmanian devils have brownish-black fur and white markings on their chests and rumps to locate one another at night. Their powerful jaws contain molar teeth capable of crushing bone.

Danger Factor

The Tasmanian devil's bite is as strong as that of a dog over three times its weight. They often wrestle with and bite one another. If a Tasmanian devil gets really angry, its ears turn red! Although they do not attack humans often, they can certainly do some damage if they feel threatened. Injuries can include severe bites and scratches, which may become infected. Trying to hug these fierce creatures is not recommended!

Conservation Status

ENDANGERED

The Tasmanian devil population began to decrease due to a disease called devil facial tumor disease, thought to be transmitted when devils bite each other. Large lumps appear on their head and mouth, making it impossible for them to eat. Thousands of devils have starved to death this way, endangering their species' survival.

What They Eat

The largest carnivorous marsupial, a devil will eat an entire mammal, including the bones and fur! They most often feed on carrion instead of hunting for themselves. When hunting for fresh food, they prey on frogs, insects, birds, and fish.

Where They Live

Hundreds of years ago, the Tasmanian devil lived throughout mainland Australia, but now it is only found on the Australian island of Tasmania. Researchers believe that they disappeared from the mainland around 3,000 to 4,000 years ago, when predatory dingoes arrived from southern Asia. Usually solitary, they live alone in hollow logs, caves, and abandoned burrows in scrublands and forests.

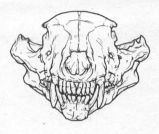

FUN FACTS

◆ Tasmanian devils will travel up to 10 miles (16 km) per day to find food, using their keen sense of smell.

◆ Ew! Like a skunk, a Tasmanian devil can release a foul-smelling gas to scare off threats.

◆ When fighting one another, Tasmanian devils may sneeze in their opponent's face. That's one way to get someone to back off!

◆ Their species name means "meat lover."

TIGER PUFFERFISH

Takifugu rubripes

(tacky-foo-goo rube-ripes)

B each ball or fish? About 31 inches (78 cm) long, the tiger pufferfish looks pretty ordinary as it slowly swims along the seabed, but when it gets scared, it can quickly pump water into its stomach, "puffing" up like a balloon. This usually deters animal predators, who leave it alone to find something easier to eat.

Danger Factor

The tiger pufferfish's liver contains the same neurotoxin as the southern blue-ringed octopus (page 110), which can cause paralysis and trouble breathing in animals and humans that consume it. Despite its deadly nature, humans eat the pufferfish as an expensive dish called "fugu." If a chef does not carefully slice away all its dangerous parts, it can be disastrous for the diner. In fact, the tiger pufferfish caused nearly 50 deaths between 1983 and 1992.

Conservation Status

NEAR THREATENED

Demand for this deadly dish threatens the tiger pufferfish's survival. Up to 11,000 tons (10,000 metric tons) of fugu are consumed each year. For the past few decades, overfishing through a method called "longline fishing" has greatly affected the number of wild pufferfish.

What They Eat

With their four-toothed beaks, tiger pufferfish crack open shellfish, such as clams and mussels. They also eat algae and marine invertebrates. Researchers believe that the tiger pufferfish gets its poison from eating prey that contains toxic bacteria, which the pufferfish is able to store safely inside its own body.

Where They Live

These living beach balls can be found in the Sea of Japan, the East China Sea, and the Yellow Sea. Clumsy swimmers, they usually hang out along the seabed, anywhere from 30 to 400 feet (9 to 120 m) below the surface.

FUN FACTS

◆ The ocean sunfish, featured in *A Curious Collection of Peculiar Creatures*, is a close relative of the tiger pufferfish.

◆ Historians have found fugu remains, or "shell mounds," in Japan—evidence that people living there ate fugu over 10,000 years ago.

◆ Cases of pufferfish poisoning were even recorded back in Ancient Egypt!

TITAN TRIGGERFISH

Balistoides viridescens

(bal-is-toy-ds veer-uh-des-ens)

Also called the "moustache triggerfish," the titan triggerfish is a brightly colored, scaly fish measuring 30 inches (75 cm) long. Its blue chin and lips are highlighted by a black line above the lip—its "moustache." When frightened or threatened, it can raise and lock its large and very sharp dorsal fin in place with a smaller "trigger" fin. Triggerfish raise their fins to anchor themselves in place when they are in rocks or crevices and to protect themselves against predators.

Danger Factor

While not venomous, this fish has a strong and damaging bite. If a scuba diver accidentally swims into a titan triggerfish's territory, the fish will attack. Injuries can range from tears in a diver's gear, bumps, and bruises to more serious damage, like divers being knocked out or having their ears bitten off! These fish can also be dangerous if eaten because they can have a toxin called "ciguatoxin," which they absorb through eating marine algae. Although harmless to the triggerfish, the toxin can be fatal to humans who consume the fish.

Conservation Status

NOT EVALUATED

Scientists do not have data on the population numbers of the titan triggerfish. Because of the fish's defense mechanism, it does not face many natural threats or predators. However, as with all coral reef fish, climate change and water pollution affect its habitat.

What They Eat

The titan triggerfish's powerful teeth are designed to crack through sea urchin and crab shells. When hunting tube worms, the fish uses its fins to dig in the sand. Titan triggerfish also snack on bits of coral and algae.

Where They Live

Among the lagoons and reefs of the central Pacific and Indian Oceans, the titan triggerfish lives around Australia, Thailand, Indonesia, and Fiji. It tends to hang out in the flatter parts of the reefs, usually no more than 160 feet (40 m) from the surface.

FUN FACTS

◆ Titan triggerfish will sometimes bite at a scuba diver's or snorkeler's swim fins while pushing them away from its territory.

◆ Triggerfish territories extend vertically, in a cone shape from seabed to surface, rather than horizontally.

◆ If you find yourself in a titan triggerfish's territory, you must swim horizontally, not toward the surface, to escape.

◆ Each of its eyes can move independently!

VAMPIRE BAT

Desmodus rotundus

(des-mo-dus ro-tun-dus)

Out in the night sky, the vampire bat's large, pointy ears can detect the breath of a sleeping animal, and its pinkish, flat, leaf-shaped nose has heat sensors that can sniff out the animal's warm blood. At 3 inches (7 cm), its body is barely the size of an adult's thumb, and even with a 7-inch (17 cm) wingspan, it weighs only about 2 ounces (56 g), allowing this brown, furry bat to climb onto its sleeping prey without waking it up.

Conservation Status

LEAST CONCERN

The vampire bat's range is wide and it adapts easily to its surroundings, so any changes to its habitat do not affect it as much as those same changes might affect other animals. Its biggest threat is humans. Farmers consider these bats a nuisance because they can infect livestock with rabies.

Where They Live

Found mostly in Brazil, vampire bats live in the warm, humid climates of Mexico and Central and South America. During the day, 20 to 100 (or more!) bats roost upside down in dark spaces like caves, old water wells, and empty mines.

FUN FACTS

◆ Digested blood smells like ammonia, so if you enter a cave where vampire bats live, you will be overpowered by a strong chemical stench.

◆ For the first month of its life, a baby vampire bat drinks its mother's milk. Then it transitions to a blood diet.

◆ Protein in the vampire bat's saliva both numbs its victim's wound and stops the blood from clotting, so they can drink as much as they need.

Danger Factor

While the nocturnal vampire bat does drink blood, its victims are usually sleeping cattle and livestock, not humans. Its sharp fangs cut a small flap in the animal's skin, and it laps at the blood with its grooved tongue. In the extremely rare cases when it bites a human, the danger is not loss of blood but the possibility of infection.

What They Eat

Can you imagine taking 30 minutes to drink 1 spoonful of water? That's how long it takes the vampire bat to drink a spoonful of blood! After only 2 tablespoons, it is so full, it can barely fly. But it has to have blood every 2 days or it will die.

WOLVERINE

Gulo gulo
(g-youl-o g-youl-o)

The largest member of the weasel family, at about 40 pounds (18 kg) and 4 feet (1.2 m) long, the wolverine has been known to pick fights with much larger animals. This muscular creature has a fierce reputation for taking whatever it wants, ripping prey apart with its incredibly sharp claws. Definitely not a creature you want to come across in the wild!

Danger Factor

Serious attitude, intelligence, and bone-crushing jaws make the wolverine an excellent villain. Like the Tasmanian devil (page 114), wolverines can put on a ferocious display in the face of larger competing predators. They do not randomly attack humans, but they do outsmart them! Wolverines have been known to spring a hunter's trap by dropping a stick in it and then stealing the bait. Researchers have even observed them moving traps and burying them.

Conservation Status

LEAST CONCERN

Decades ago, people hunted the wolverine for its fur. Now, farmers who blame them for preying on livestock will poison and kill them. Although their number is decreasing in some places, conservationists are not concerned about the wolverine's overall population.

What They Eat

This omnivore eats a variety of plants and animals, including rabbits, squirrels, and even reindeer. A wolverine will scavenge carrion, steal from hunting traps, and raid hibernating animals' dens. It uses snow like a refrigerator, burying its leftovers and then spraying its scent to mark its territory.

Where They Live

Wolverines are not easy for us to see, as they keep to remote evergreen forests, taiga, and tundra biomes in the cold and polar climates of the most northern parts of Asia, Europe, and North America. They make beds of grass and leaves in small caves, rock piles, or abandoned burrows.

FUN FACTS

◆ The wolverine's scientific name, *Gulo gulo*, comes from the Latin word for "glutton," a person or animal who overeats.

◆ A baby wolverine, called a "kit," lives with its mother until it is two years old. Dad comes for playdates and to teach it how to hunt.

◆ This wild animal inspired the famously dangerous Marvel character of the same name.

◆ Researchers put a GPS collar on a wolverine to track it. In just two months, the wolverine walked over 500 miles (800 km)!

◆ A wolverine has built-in "snowshoes"—foot pads that spread out to twice the size of their feet to help them stay on top of snow.

YELLOW FEVER MOSQUITO

Aedes aegypti
(ay-ee-dees egypt-eye)

At first glance, most mosquitoes look the same, but if you get up close and personal, you begin to see what makes the yellow fever mosquito unique. Barely three quarters of an inch (2 cm) long, it has white, curvy scales on the back of its black thorax and three pairs of legs. Its elongated mouth includes a stinger-like proboscis, which, in the case of female mosquitoes, is ideal for drinking blood. The female's ability to spread illness far and wide during her one-month adult life makes this mosquito especially dangerous.

Danger Factor

Female yellow fever mosquitoes can carry several diseases, such as yellow fever, dengue, and Zika virus. Symptoms of these diseases include headaches, body aches, vomiting, jaundice, fever, organ failure, and possible death. Researchers estimate that 1 million deaths are caused by mosquitoes every year, and the yellow fever mosquito is responsible for most of them.

Conservation Status

GLOBALLY INVASIVE

Health officials are trying to limit the population of yellow fever mosquitoes because the viruses they transmit are so destructive to communities around the world. But it's important to remember that even pests have a place in the ecosystem. All species of mosquito play a role in the environment, by pollinating fruits and flowers or by being a food source for other animals, such as bats, frogs, and fish.

What They Eat

Mosquito larvae eat plankton, algae, and bacteria found in their aquatic habitat. All adult mosquitoes feed on nectar and fruit juice. Females suck blood from humans and other animals because their eggs need the protein in order to develop.

Where They Live

Hundreds of years ago, the yellow fever mosquito spread out from Africa to other tropical and subtropical regions. It can now be found in South and Central America, as well as Mexico and parts of the southern United States. The mosquito can survive in any area with humidity.

FUN FACTS

◆ Do mosquitoes think you're sweet? It may be your blood type. Female mosquitoes have shown a preference for people with type O blood.

◆ A mosquito's buzz is not caused by flapping wings. Instead, a small organ at the base of its wings scrapes against the mosquito while it flies. This is also a way for mosquitoes to talk to one another.

◆ In 1951, Dr. Max Theiler, an expert in tropical medicine, received a Nobel Prize for a vaccine against yellow fever that he created in 1937. So far, it is the only time a Nobel Prize has been awarded for the invention of a vaccine.

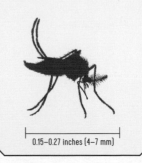

0.15–0.27 inches (4–7 mm)

RESOURCES

Many of the animals in this book are endangered; they need our help. Here are leading organizations dedicated to protecting our planet and its precious wildlife. Get involved and help save your favorite dangerous creatures!

World Wildlife Fund
worldwildlife.org

Oceana
oceana.org

Wildlife Conservation Society
wcs.org

The Sierra Club
sierraclub.org

Conservation International
conservation.org

International Fund for Animal Welfare
ifaw.org

Defenders of Wildlife
defenders.org

International Union for Conservation of Nature
iucn.org

International Animal Rescue
internationalanimalrescue.org

The Nature Conservancy
nature.org

ABOUT THE AUTHOR

The author of *A Curious Collection of Peculiar Creatures,* **SAMI BAYLY** completed her degree in natural history illustration at the University of Newcastle. She's drawn to the weird and wonderful—finding the beauty and importance in all living things, regardless of their appearance—and is eager to share her appreciation with others. *A Curious Collection of Dangerous Creatures* is her second book. She lives in Armidale, New South Wales, Australia.

samibayly.com | @samibayly

The Experiment, LLC
220 East 23rd Street, Suite 600
New York, NY 10001-4658
theexperimentpublishing.com

THE EXPERIMENT and its colophon are registered trademarks of The Experiment, LLC. Many of the designations used by manufacturers and sellers to distinguish their products are claimed as trademarks. Where those designations appear in this book and The Experiment was aware of a trademark claim, the designations have been capitalized.

The Experiment's books are available at special discounts when purchased in bulk for premiums and sales promotions as well as for fundraising or educational use. For details, contact us at info@theexperimentpublishing.com.

Library of Congress Cataloging-in-Publication Data

Names: Bayly, Sami, author.
Title: A curious collection of dangerous creatures : an illustrated
   encyclopedia / Sami Bayly.
Description: New York : The Experiment, 2021. | Audience: Ages 8 to 14 |
   Audience: Grades 4-6
Identifiers: LCCN 2021030509 (print) | LCCN 2021030510 (ebook) | ISBN
   9781615198245 (hardcover) | ISBN 9781615198252 (ebook)
Subjects: LCSH: Dangerous animals--Encyclopedias, Juvenile.
Classification: LCC QL100 .B39 2021 (print) | LCC QL100 (ebook) | DDC
   591.6/5--dc23
LC record available at https://lccn.loc.gov/2021030509
LC ebook record available at https://lccn.loc.gov/2021030510

ISBN 978-1-61519-824-5
Ebook ISBN 978-1-61519-825-2

Cover and text design by Jack Dunnington

Manufactured in China

First printing November 2021
10 9 8 7 6 5 4 3 2 1